More ABSOLUTE BEGINNER'S Guides

The Absolute Beginner's Guide to Taking Great Photos

The Absolute Beginner's Guide to Buying a House

The Absolute Beginner's Cookbook, Revised 3rd Edition

The Absolute Beginner's Guide to MIXING DRINKS

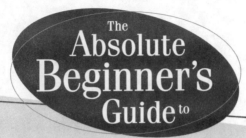

MIXING DRINKS

Bev Bennett

PRIMA PUBLISHING

Copyright © 2002 by Prima Publishing, a division of Random House, Inc.

Published by Prima Publishing, Roseville, California. Member of the Crown Publishing Group, a division of Random House, Inc.

PRIMA PUBLISHING and colophon are trademarks of Random House, Inc., registered with the United States Patent and Trademark Office.

Interior design by Susan Sugnet, Prima Design Group

Library of Congress Cataloging-in-Publication Data on File

ISBN: 0-7615-3616-7

02 03 04 05 06 HH 10 9 8 7 6 5 4 3 2 1
Printed in the United States of America

First Edition

Visit us online at www.primapublishing.com

To my husband, Linn,
and a special toast to my daughter, Rebecca,
and my son, Ben,
for their encouragement, participation,
and wonderful feedback.

Contents

Acknowledgments

What started as a ritual of after-work Margaritas with my buddies blossomed into a lifelong appreciation of cocktails. I treasure the memories of friends and laughter.

Thanks to my agent, Grace Freedson, I've been able to recall how much pleasure I've experienced. Her skills, patience, and encouragement are to be treasured.

My husband, Linn, and children, Rebecca and Ben, spent many dinner hours listening to the whir of a blender. They went thirsty when I determined that the drink I was making wasn't right for sipping. Who but family would wait an hour for the perfected version of Caribbean Breeze, a two-minute drink that combines banana, coconut, and pineapple? Okay guys . . . you can drink now.

Rebecca and Ben know I'm much more comfortable with a measuring cup than a computer program, so they deserve extra praise for their technical support. And thanks, Rebecca, for your phrase "ambient-techno-jazz." I'll use it at my next cocktail party.

The editors at Prima are ideal: supportive, smart, enthusiastic, and focused. I'd like to single out Denise Sternad, my acquisitions editor, and Michelle McCormack, my project editor, for special thanks. Rosaleen Bertolino is more than a copyeditor—she works miracles with words.

My dear friend Kim Upton, who always knows what to say and what to serve, deserves a cheer for sharing the recipe for Havana Delight.

And to the gang that used to haunt Su Casa, a round of Margaritas every Friday night.

The Absolute
Beginner's Guide to
MIXING DRINKS

Let's Get Out the Jigger

An Introduction to the
Delights of Drink Making

You wouldn't think you'd need a book to tell you how to mix a drink—and a beginner's book at that, would you? Heck, no. You've been gleefully sipping cocktails from the day you turned twenty-one. You know who serves the tangiest Sour Apple Martini in town; you know the lyrics to every Frank Sinatra song worth drinking to, and you think a cocktail glass should win an award for architectural design.

But truth or dare here . . . do you know how to make a great Daiquiri, Martini, or Cosmopolitan? Do you always reach for the appropriate glass when you pour a Screwdriver? Probably not. And you're not alone, so don't feel embarrassed. After all, drink mixing isn't as regular a part of your daily routine as, let's say, pouring milk on your breakfast cornflakes. Fortunately, drink mixing is one of the easiest and most enjoyable skills you can acquire as an adult. You'll find that your talents pay off. Your friends will surround you, eager to benefit from your drink-making abilities.

Too bad there's so much confusion and lack of basic information getting in your way. This book eliminates all that.

Most drink books assume you know the taste difference between gin and vodka. This book doesn't make any such assumptions. Most books don't tell you what kind of glass to use for each drink. This book does. Most books don't tell you it's fun to mix drinks. This book does. That's why you need this book.

GETTING IN THE MIX

Mixing your first drink is a rite of passage. It's your entry into a secret language in which the word "dry" refers to a wet drink and "sour" means sweet with a tingle. You'll have toys at your disposal, from elegant spoons with twisted handles to turbo blenders that churn ice into powder in minutes. Who said kids have all the fun? As an adult you can share good times and a fine cocktail with your friends. Having a drink is something grown-ups do.

Do you remember being sent to bed as a child, when your parents had company? The grown-ups were downstairs having a ball while you were supposedly asleep. But inevitably the laughter reached such a crescendo you had to tiptoe to the staircase and see what the commotion was all about. It was party time. Your folks were transformed from the irritating scolds you knew into lively, funny people. You heard ice clinking in glasses and the rush of club soda being poured. Everyone was congenial. Boy, did you want to join that party.

Now you're an adult and you can.

I recall the urge to enter this cocktail society when I turned twenty-one. My inspiration, however, dated back further than my parents. I wanted to live like Dorothy Parker, who reigned over New York's literary scene during the 1920s. Parker and other literary lights—Robert Benchley; Harold Ross, who started the *New Yorker* magazine; and Alexander Woollcott—were regulars at Manhattan's Algonquin Hotel. Their humor was so sharp and biting, their victims called them the "vicious circle." Perhaps liquor loosened their tongues. It's hard to know. Historians write that they were not only prodigious drinkers, but during the height of Prohibition, they reveled in their vices. It was Parker who wrote:

> *I like to have a Martini,*
> *Two at the very most.*
> *After three I'm under the table,*
> *After four I'm under the host.*

I could well imagine myself as a bubbling fountain of bons mots, amusing my adoring friends, all the while sipping my oversized Martini in a gold-rimmed glass. I had the fantasy down pat. A college graduate with a lease on a studio apartment slightly bigger than my dorm room, I was on my way to a decadent life as a food writer and Martini fanatic. I wasn't about to be stopped by the fact that my furniture consisted of a sleeper sofa, one table, and one lamp or that my refrigerator fit under the kitchen counter. As long as the freezer compartment was cold enough to freeze water and the refrigerator would hold a few bottles, I had the makings of a cocktail hostess.

Fun Fact!

Despite Martini mania, America's most popular cocktail is the Bloody Mary according to food writer Sharon Tyler Herbst.

I slowly filled the kitchen shelves with glasses from secondhand shops—cocktail, sherry, cordial glasses. I loved the fine, fragile stems and thin glass bowls. I'd sip my morning orange juice in a cranberry-tinted highball glass. In the evening I'd have a little soda in my champagne flute. I even collected a great stock of bar lines—until I developed my own, of course. One of my favorites was Benchley's quip: "Why don't you get out of that wet coat and into a dry Martini."

There was one critical drawback to my envisioned life. I didn't know how to make a drink. I'd never even tasted a Martini. Sure, I could pour beer. It was impossible to get through four years of college without mastering a perfect head of foam. But Martinis? Manhattans? You may as well have been talking brain surgery. This wasn't like passing along the heirloom turkey-stuffing recipe. Parents didn't tell their daughters how to make drinks.

There weren't a lot of guides available either. Parker and the gang talked about drinking but they never told readers how to make a cocktail. How did the drink-challenged people of my generation acquire their skills?

Like any sensible single young woman setting up house-keeping, I turned to the culinary bible, *The Joy of Cooking,* for an answer. And, to my delight and surprise, there, in black and white, was a Martini recipe: 1 to 2 jiggers dry vermouth, 6 to 7 jiggers gin, a twist of lemon or a small seeded olive. I mixed the ingredients, poured the concoction into my best cocktail glass and sipped, and sipped, and sipped. I hadn't read the introduction, which explained the recipe served four.

Ouch. That first hangover. It took days for my head to stop ringing. I learned two valuable lessons: Never drink to excess and always read directions thoroughly before beginning any project. It was the first and last time I consumed so much liquor in one sitting, but it was the first of many experiments.

Every time I went to a restaurant, I'd skip the usual beer or white wine and ask for the house cocktail. I perused bartenders' shelves the way some women go through the clothing racks at Bloomingdale's. I was looking for clues to what

> **Fun Fact!**
>
> If someone tells you he's not drinking very much—just a "nip"—you may roll your eyes. The British term refers to a half-pint or one-cup measure.

made bartenders' drinks so marvelous. I still yearned to become a cocktail maven.

And then one evening I had an unforeseen opportunity. I went to a movie with a group of friends. Afterward we couldn't settle on a place to go for a drink. Taking a deep breath, I invited everyone to my place. I tossed pillows on the floor, wiped the dust from my odd assortment of glasses, and doubled my *Joy of Cooking* Martini recipe to serve eight.

It worked. There we were sitting around in my sparse surroundings — laughing, glasses clinking, feeling very convivial. It wasn't elegant; it was fabulous fun, and at last I knew what I wanted from the cocktail culture. I wasn't going to become the next Dorothy Parker. I was going to make my friends feel at ease with the best drink I could mix.

Over the years I honed my skills—sometimes as the result of embarrassing trial and error—to the point where I now feel confident trying any cocktail. And if I don't know how to make a drink, I'll experiment until I get it right.

> **Helpful Hint**
>
> A "call" in bartender lingo refers to a brand-name alcohol. Usually you'll be served the "house" or "bar" brand unless you specify a certain brand of liquor in your cocktail. When you entertain, note your friends' preferences in spirits. Next time you shop, choose those brands for entertaining.

As you read this book and try the recipes, you, too, will enjoy the research and have the pleasure of mastering a skill. If you can laugh at the occasional blunder that you are likely to make, as well as triumph in your achievements, I'll consider *The Absolute Beginner's Guide to Mixing Drinks* a great success.

You're about to join the thousands of people who are cocktail connoisseurs. "It's a sign of Americans' conviviality that cocktails are so inventive and so cleverly named," wrote H. L. Mencken. Americans, for example, renamed the

English whiskey-and-soda a "highball," with its colorful allusion to railroad lore. Mixed drinks have a long history. You'll find the word "cocktail" refers to a drink in early nineteenth century writings. A Kentucky breakfast of the 1800s was described as "three cocktails and a chaw of terbacker," according to food writer Waverly Root. And yes, historians give the United States credit for creating cocktails. The British Isles contributed Scotch and Irish whiskey; France, wine; and America gave the world cocktails. Drinks such as the Martini, Screwdriver, and Bloody Mary, are as ingrained in American culture as blue jeans and ice cream.

> ## Fun Fact!
>
> Americans can thank their northern neighbors for keeping a steady supply of whiskey flowing south during Prohibition. It was the introduction of Canadian whisky in the 1920s that launched its popularity in the United States.

Even the restrictions of a national alcohol Prohibition in the 1920s and early 1930s couldn't dim the thirst for a mixed drink. Ironically some of the best-loved mixed drinks originated or gained popularity during Prohibition, when people added flavorings to disguise the taste of "bathtub gin," which would otherwise be unpalatable. Women influenced cocktail society during Prohibition. Instead of going to public bars, people drank in private clubs or in homes where women served liquor in cocktails, not straight drinks.

You'll find many definitions for cocktails. Cocktails are usually considered to be a liquor and flavorings that can include juice, bitters, tonic water, club soda, or another alcoholic beverage. But cocktails don't even need to have alcohol. Dress up a drink with enough accessories, pack it in a pretty glass, give it attitude, and it's a cocktail. A tall lemonade isn't a cocktail; lemonade in a highball glass with a cherry and a wheel of lemon sure is.

Bartenders certainly have been cocktail visionaries. Imagine someone taking the first sip of a Bloody Mary. Vodka and tomato juice—what an unlikely and absolutely delicious combination! The professionals still lead the way, introducing consumers to ever more exotic concoctions each year.

But now you, too, can become a mixologist, a fancy way of saying you've got the skills to make a mixed drink. *The Absolute Beginner's Guide to Mixing Drinks* will help you develop your mixology craft. It's never the last call, so let's get out the jigger.

2

The Spirits Move You

The Basics of Stocking Your Bar

You're inspired. You've come from a delightful evening at a restaurant where the bartender dazzled your taste buds with an original and potent creation. Or maybe a party transported you to an era of gin and Gershwin. Now that you've been seduced by the cocktail mystique—one part romance, one part style, and one part great flavor—you're ready to share the magic.

In this chapter, you'll learn the absolute basics of making a good drink. You'll learn about the liquors that form a backdrop to bars. You'll get a mini profile of the standard spirits from anisette to whiskey, or whisky, if you prefer. Even if you've never tasted aquavit or can't distinguish Cointreau from Triple Sec, you'll learn how to serve each spirit.

 ## ALCOHOL FROM A TO Z

Imagine the surprise of the first man or woman who accidentally sipped a mixture of fermented grains and rainwater. It must have been a raw, fiery brew, but one with enough lingering and pleasant associations to keep us perfecting our grain-distilling techniques ever since.

You'll see only a fraction of the distiller's creativity in your local liquor store. Although a handful of spirits—brandy, gin, rum, tequila, vodka, and whiskey—constitute the main ingredients for most of the cocktails you'll ever make, thousands are available worldwide. And distillers make new ones every year.

No doubt you know some things about liquor already. You may specify a certain brand of vodka when you go out for cocktails. But there's more to liquor. For the fun, the history, and the flavor, read on. You'll read who took the *e* out of "whiskey," which liquor tastes like rye bread, and how you can substitute one spirit for another in cocktail recipes.

> **Fun Fact!**
>
> You won't find spirits higher than 190 proof. Any more alcohol and the beverage draws moisture from the air and begins to dilute.

Amaretto: An almond-flavored, amber-colored liqueur that originated in Italy.

Taste: Nutty, like almonds. Some versions are very sweet while others are slightly drier.

Drink use: Straight as an after-dinner drink, in place of whiskey in a Whiskey Sour, or as a layer in a Pousse-Café.

Substitute: Crème d'amande.

Anisette: A clear liqueur made from aniseeds. Anisette was developed as a safe alternative to absinthe, a liquor infused with toxic wormwood and banned in many parts of the world.

Taste: Anise or licorice flavor.

Drink use: Straight or mixed with water as an aperitif or an after-dinner digestive.

Substitute: Pastis, sambuca, Goldwasser, or ouzo.

Applejack: An American-made apple brandy produced by distilling fermented apple juice.

Taste: Depending on the brand, applejack may be sweet, dry, or just plain rough. The apple taste may be subtle or pronounced.

Drink use: Sour Apple Martini, Mulled Cider, or punch.

Substitute: Calvados (see entry).

Apricot brandy: A brandy distilled from apricots, often made from apricot juice.

Taste: Dry with a strong, fruity aroma and flavor.

Drink use: As a layer in a Pousse-Café, as a substitute for whiskey in a Whiskey Sour, or straight as an after-dinner drink.

Substitute: Peach brandy.

Aquavit: A clear Scandinavian spirit distilled from grains or potatoes.

Taste: Slightly sweet with hints of caraway seed, fennel seed, and aniseed. Different brands accent different seed tastes. And yes, it does taste like a good Scandinavian rye bread. It should always be served well-chilled for the best flavor.

Drink use: Straight as an aperitif or in a Martini.

Substitute: Aquavit is unique.

Armagnac: A brandy from southwestern France.

Taste: Depending on the producer, Armagnac can be raw and fiery or have great finesse like an aged Cognac. It may have a hint of the oak barrels in which it is aged. At its best, its perfume seduces the most jaded drinker.

Drink use: Straight, in hot coffee.

Substitute: Cognac.

Beer: A brewed beverage that is generally made from malt, hops, and water and fermented with yeast. In some parts of the world, such as Japan, beer is made from rice. In most areas, barley is turned into malt to produce beer. Different ingredients and brewing styles result in beers with varying body, color, flavor, and aroma.

Taste: Depending on the style and ingredients, beer can be sweet, rich, mellow, or chocolate-like. Or it can be thin, watery, and unsubstantial tasting.

Drink use: Straight or in Black Velvet.

Substitute: Beer is unique.

> **Fun Fact!**
>
> If you order a brew in an English pub you may be shocked that the beer isn't ice cold. Chilling doesn't necessarily improve the flavor of beer. Complex-tasting English lagers, ales, and porters are served at higher temperatures—ranging from 50 to 60 degrees Fahrenheit—to bring out the flavor. A light, bland-tasting American beer can be served ice cold.

Benedictine: A honey-colored French liqueur.

Taste: Herbal and honey-like.

Drink use: As a layer in a Pousse-Café; straight, or on the rocks as an after-dinner drink.

Substitute: B & B, a combination of Benedictine and brandy. It has a similar taste but isn't as sweet.

Bourbon: A type of American whiskey named for Bourbon, Kentucky, where it originated. It was originally made from corn in Bourbon County, Kentucky. It starts with a fermented mash that's at least 51 percent corn, usually mixed with rye and barley. Bourbon is aged from two to twelve years in oak barrels to develop its character and appealing caramel color.

> **Fun Fact!**
>
> The word "brandy" comes from the Dutch "brandewijn," which means burnt wine.

Taste: Slightly smoky and mellow.

Drink use: Neat, over ice, or in a Mint Julep.
Substitute: Straight whiskey.

Brandy: A distilled product of the grape, such as Armagnac or Cognac. Many countries have their own versions of brandy. But brandy goes beyond grapes. Other fruits can also be distilled into brandies. One example is the French apple brandy Calvados (which has its own entry in this section).
Taste: So much depends on the distilling process. If well-refined, brandy can be a fine, aged Cognac, silken as it slides down your throat, or it can be a cheap product that sets your stomach on fire.
Drink use: Straight, fruit-based cocktails, or in a cup of coffee.
Substitute: Cognac or Armagnac.

Calvados: A clear apple brandy distilled in Normandy, France.
Taste: Like an aged brandy with a perfumed apple scent.
Drink use: Straight, in place of applejack in a Sour Apple Martini.
Substitute: Applejack or eau-de-vie de cidre (an apple brandy or spirit).

Campari: A spirit flavored with herbs and orange peel.
Taste: Campari is available in bitter or sweet versions. The bitter is intended to whet the appetite.
Drink use: Campari and soda and Canadian and Campari.
Substitute: Campari is unique.

Cassis; crème de cassis: A syrupy, red liqueur made from black currants. Cassis is made in various parts of France, but the highest quality comes from the northeastern region.
Taste: Sweet, fruity.
Drink use: Kir, Kir Royale.
Substitute: Other fruit liqueurs such as crème de framboise for a slightly different taste.

Champagne: A sparkling wine, usually white, from the Champagne province of France. That's the dry version. To fully describe champagne, imagine tickling, tantalizing bubbles that create a celebration in your mouth. It's the thirst-quenching alternative to a confetti-strewn party.

Taste: From crisp and dry to fruity white wine, depending on the variety.

Drink use: Straight, Kir Royale, Champagne Cocktail, Mimosa, and Bellini.

Substitute: American, Spanish, or Italian sparkling wines. Spanish and Italian sparkling wines will probably be on the sweet side.

> **Helpful Hint**
>
> When you see the word "crème" on a liqueur, it means the product has been sweetened. Expect a syrupy, sweet drink. In addition to crème de cassis, you'll find such popular liqueurs as crème de cacao, crème de menthe, and crème de banana in stores.

Cherry Heering; Peter Heering: A cherry liqueur made in Denmark. This product uses a large proportion of cherry stones in the distilling process. The resulting liqueur is lighter and less cloying than some fruit liqueurs. You're more likely to see it packaged as Peter Heering.

Taste: Strong cherry flavor without being too sweet.

Drink use: Fruit punch or try it in a Daiquiri, Cherry-Orange Delight, Chocolate-Cream Cherry.

Substitute: Cherry brandy.

Cognac: A brandy distilled from the wine of certain grape varieties in the Cognac region of France. Cognac is distinguished by its age and finesse.

Taste: The youngest Cognac is raw tasting with a strong hint of grapes. As it ages Cognac becomes smoother, oaken or buttery tasting, depending on the age and the treatment.

Drink use: Young Cognac may be mixed with soda; straight for aged Cognac.

Substitute: Brandy.

Cointreau: A clear liqueur made from oranges.
Taste: Slightly sharp orange taste; clean, not too sweet.
Drink use: Sidecar, Between the Sheets.
Substitute: Grand Marnier or Triple Sec.

Curaçao: A Dutch liqueur made from orange skins grown on the island of Curaçao. Curaçao is generic and there are several types. It comes in clear or blue.
Taste: A definite orange flavor.
Drink use: Straight or substitute for Triple Sec in a Margarita.
Substitute: Cointreau, Grand Marnier, Triple Sec.

Dessert wine: A wine with a high percentage of sugar. You may have the impression that sweet wines are "cheap" and that you should only drink dry varieties—not!
Taste: The best-quality dessert wines, such as the French Sauternes, taste like citrus and honey.
Drink use: Serve with or instead of dessert.
Substitute: Dessert wines are unique.

Drambuie: A Scottish honey-based liqueur with a golden color.
Taste: Honey-sweet and slightly herbal.
Drink use: Straight or on the rocks as an after-dinner drink. It's essential to a Rusty Nail (see chapter 4).
Substitute: Drambuie is unique, but you may want to experiment with Benedictine in mixed drinks.

Dubonnet: A French aperitif made from wine, bitters, and quinine. Dubonnet comes in red, which is more full-bodied and sweet, and white, which is dry.
Taste: Slightly herbal and bitter.
Drink use: Straight, on the rocks, or with soda.
Substitute: Dry vermouth, in either red or white, depending on the drink use.

Frangelico: An Italian hazelnut liqueur with a hazelnut color.
Taste: Nutty and slightly honey-like.

Drink use: As a layer in a Pousse-Café or straight. It can also be mixed with cream as a dessert drink: 1½ ounces (3 tablespoons) Frangelico to ½ ounce (1 tablespoon) cream.

Substitute: Try another nut liqueur, such as praline, which is pecan-based.

Galliano: An Italian herb- and spice-based liqueur with an intense yellow color.

Taste: Sweet with a hint of herbs.

Drink use: Straight as an after-dinner drink, as a layer in a Pousse-Café, or in its most famous incarnation, in the drink of the 1970s—the Harvey Wallbanger (see chapter 4).

Substitute: Galliano is unique.

Gin: A clear spirit made from the distillation of grain spirits of malted barley and rye, or of corn and flavored with juniper berries. There are two basic gin styles: British, which has a higher proof and is dry, and Holland, which is less alcoholic and aged.

Taste: A woodsy or herbal hint from the juniper berries and other botanicals that may be added.

Drink use: Martini, Gin and Tonic, Gin Fizz, Gin Gimlet, and Tom Collins.

Substitute: Vodka, but only in a drink that uses a large proportion of mixer, such as a Gin and Tonic.

Godiva Chocolate Liqueur: A brand-name liqueur.

Taste: Sweet, well-defined chocolate flavor.

Drink use: Straight as an after-dinner drink or mixed with cream as a dessert drink: Mix 1½ ounces (3 tablespoons) Godiva to ½ ounce (1 tablespoon)

> **Fun Fact!**
>
> Gin may have been one of the earliest of the "herbal dietary supplements." During the 1700s, a "medication" of alcohol and juniper berries was prescribed for sluggish appetites. Some people still swear by a therapeutic gin drink before dinner.

cream. The liqueur can also be used in a Chocotini or as a layer in a Pousse-Café.

Substitute: Crème de cacao.

Grappa: A potent Italian spirit made from grape skins.

Taste: Depending on the manufacturer, grappa can be a fiery, "grab-your-throat" kind of spirit or refined and almost mellow.

Drink use: Straight as an after-dinner drink.

Substitute: Armagnac.

Madeira: A fortified wine from the Portuguese island of Madeira.

Taste: Like sherry, Madeira comes in a variety of styles, from light and dry to full and rich.

Drink use: Serve as an aperitif or an after-dinner drink.

Substitute: Madeira is unique.

Midori: A melon-flavored liqueur with a light green color.

Taste: A hint of honeydew melon, a subtle fruit flavor.

Drink use: Use Midori in place of Triple Sec in a Margarita.

Substitute: Midori is unique.

Port: A Portuguese wine fortified with the addition of Portuguese grape brandy.

Taste: Rich berry, a hint of vanilla, a slight scent of oak, a touch of honey.

Drink use: Straight, Sangria.

Substitute: Port is unique, though you can use sherry for some drinks.

Rum: A spirit made from fermented sugarcane. Most fine rums come from molasses, but may also be made directly from sugarcane juice. Ranges from clear to amber to rich brown color.

Taste: Light rums have a hint of sweetness and a slight perfumed aroma. The lighter the rum the more subtle the taste. Dark rums have a richer caramel flavor.

Drink use: Light rum: Daiquiri, Piña Colada, Cuba Libre. Dark rum: Planter's Punch, or try it instead of brandy in Eggnog.

Substitute: Rum is unique.

Rye: American whiskey distilled from a grain mash that's predominantly rye.

Taste: Similar to bourbon or Irish whiskey but a bit drier.

Drink use: Manhattan.

Substitute: Irish whiskey.

> **Fun Fact!**
>
> When told that General Grant drank whiskey while leading his Union Army troops, President Lincoln reportedly asked for the brand name so he could give it to his other generals.

Sake: A colorless, Japanese rice-fermented spirit, which could be classified as a beer because it's grain-based and relatively low in alcohol. However, it is served as a fortified wine.

Taste: Dry to slightly sweet; some brands have a bitter aftertaste.

Drink use: Straight and Saketini.

Substitute: Sake is unique but any sherry can substitute in cooking.

Sherry: A brandy-fortified wine from Spain. There are several styles including fino, manzanilla, amontillado, oloroso, and cream.

Taste: Depending on the style and the brand, sherry may be dry, nutty, honey-like, or rich and syrupy.

Drink use: Straight and Finotini.

Substitute: Sherry is unique.

Sloe Gin: A gin-based liqueur flavored with the small, bitter, black plumlike fruit of the blackthorn tree. Red in color.

Taste: Sweet.
Drink use: Substitute for gin in a Gin Fizz.
Substitute: Cranberry liqueur may do in a pinch.

Southern Comfort: Clear, amber-colored, bourbon-based liqueur.
Taste: Sweet and silken.
Drink use: Serve straight, on the rocks, or instead of whiskey in a Whiskey Sour.
Substitute: Southern Comfort is unique.

Strega: A yellow-colored Italian herb-based liqueur.
Taste: Very sweet.
Drink use: Straight or on the rocks as a digestive.
Substitute: Chartreuse, a French brandy-and-herb-based liqueur.

Tequila: Distilled spirits from Mexico's blue agave plant. The distillation is mixed with sugarcane and processed.
Taste: Depending on the quality and brand, the flavor may be fiery, raw, delicate, slightly smoky, or smooth.
Drink use: Margarita.
Substitute: Tequila is unique.

Triple Sec: A clear, orange-flavored liqueur.
Taste: Slightly dryer than some orange liqueurs, with definite orange character.
Drink use: Margarita (Triple Sec is the liqueur most bartenders use in their margaritas) and Sidecar.
Substitute: Cointreau, curaçao, or Grand Marnier.

Vermouth: A blend of wine, sometimes a touch of brandy, and herbs.
Taste: Two types, dry and sweet, are available. Both have a hint of herbs.
Drink use: Dry: Martini, Gibson. Sweet: Manhattan.
Substitute: Vermouth is unique.

Vodka: A spirit native to Eastern Europe, made from potatoes, or more commonly, from grain.

Taste: Neutral. For those who don't like the taste of alcohol, vodka offers the advantage of having very little flavor unless you choose one of the many fruit, spice, or herb-accented varieties on the market.

Drink use: Martini, Vodka and Tonic, Black Russian, and Bloody Mary.

Substitute: Vodka is unique.

> **Fun Fact!**
>
> The word "vermouth" comes from the German "wermut" or the Anglo-Saxon "wermod." Both mean wormwood.

Whiskey: The fermented mash of a grain that could include rye, corn, barley, oats, or wheat.

Taste: Depending on the grain, the distilling process, and aging, whiskey may be smoky, honey-like, rich, fiery, or mellow, or have a combination of characteristics.

Drink use: Straight, Whiskey Sour, Old-Fashioned, and Manhattan.

Substitute: A dry, dark or golden rum.

> **Helpful Hint**
>
> Can you use vodka and gin interchangeably in cocktails? Purists say no. Gin has a distinctive spicy touch of juniper berries; vodka is flavorless. However, you may find the spirits are equally enjoyable in some drinks, such as a Tonic or a Collins.

Wine: The fermented juice of the grape. Wine may be white, red, rose, still, sparkling, or fortified (such as port or sherry).

Taste: Depending on the grapes, growing areas, weather, and harvesting and aging techniques, wine may be dry, sweet, fruity, oaklike, tannic, or just plain sour.

Drink use: Straight, Sangria (red wine), Kir (white wine), Spritzer (white wine), and punch.

Substitute: Wine is unique.

Liqueurs

Liqueurs have a supporting though essential role in cocktails. Tequila may be the star of a Margarita, but if it weren't for Triple Sec, it would just be a strong drink. The addition of Triple Sec adds body, sweetness, and a definite orange character to a Margarita. All liqueurs have a high sugar content. Some people insist it's the sugar that leads to nasty hangovers, though there's no scientific evidence to that effect.

Liqueurs are the most complex of spirits. Benedictine is made from an ancient formula of honey and herbs. Some liqueurs are the exclusive formula of a spirits house. For example, there's only one Galliano. It comes in a tall bottle and it's unique.

However, you'll find a variety of orange- or coffee-flavored liqueurs, each with a slightly different taste. You can experiment to see if the particular liqueur a recipe calls for is essential, or if you can substitute the spirit you prefer. The following list groups liqueurs by flavor categories, which may help when you shop or mix drinks.

> **Fun Fact!**
>
> For the early settlers in Pennsylvania, whiskey proved to be an easy product. Poor roads made it nearly impossible for farmers to get their grains to market without spoilage. But if farmers allowed their crops to ferment and distilled them in pot stills, they could easily ship the liquid. In the 1700s, whiskey became an important source of income for Pennsylvanians.

Anise and licorice: Anisette, Pernod, sambuca, and Galliano.

Coffee: Kahlúa and Tia Maria.

Cream: Bailey's Irish Cream, E & J Cask & Cream.

Fruit: Crème de cassis (black currant), Chambord (raspberry), Midori (melon), and sloe gin (the sloe berry). There's also the orange group that includes Grand Marnier, Cointreau, curaçao, and Triple Sec.

Herb: Benedictine, B & B, Chartreuse, and Jägermeister.

Mint: Crème de menthe and peppermint schnapps.

Nut: Amaretto (almond), Frangelico (hazelnut), and praline (pecan) are some of the choices.

Whiskey: Drambuie, Irish Mist, and Southern Comfort.

> ### Fun Fact!
> Do you spell it whiskey or whisky? The spelling varies with the country of origin. You'll drink Canadian or Scotch whisky, but Irish whiskey. American variations—bourbon, corn, and rye—are whiskey.

STOCKING YOUR BAR

Now that you know the most common spirits available, you'll want to choose products to stock your bar. Select those liquors that suit your drinking style and those of your friends.

For example, if you like fruity, complex concoctions, you'll want rums and liqueurs in your bar; if you like simple, straightforward drinks, you'll probably want to stock up on whiskey, gin, and vodka.

You may want to buy two bottles of liquors such as bourbon, whiskey, gin, rum,

> ### Helpful Hint
> How do you use flavored vodka products such as citrus or chile vodka? Serve flavored vodka straight, over ice, or to enhance your favorite cocktail. For example, add chile-accented vodka to a Bloody Mary spiked with hot sauce. You'll find recipes for making your own flavored spirits in chapter 5.

The Absolute Beginner's Bar

For the absolute beginner's bar, include the following liquors:

Gin   Rum (light)

Vodka   Whiskey

scotch, tequila, and vodka. One line will be the highest quality for drinking straight (see The Quality Question on page 27) and the other will be more economical, for mixing. Beer and wine brands should be your personal favorites, regardless of price.

The essential bar list will get you through most drink orders. It is an investment, however, and if you'd like to start out more gradually, check The Absolute Beginner's Bar list (above).

The Essential Bar

Beer	Vermouth, dry
Bourbon	Vermouth, sweet
Gin	Vodka
Rum (light and dark)	Whiskey
Scotch	White wine
Tequila	Red wine
Triple Sec	

The Essential Mixers

You'll also want mixers. What's gin without the tonic? And a Bloody Mary without the tomato juice is pretty bloodless. Here's what you'll need to complement the spirits:

Bitters (such as angostura bitters)
Bottled sweetened lime juice (for Gin Gimlets)

The Beginner's Mixers

For the absolute beginner's mixers, include the following:

Club soda   Simple syrup

Sweet-and-sour mix   Tonic water

Club soda
Cola
Ginger ale
Grenadine
Half-and-half or cream (for those rich coffee and liqueur
    drinks)
Orange juice
Simple syrup (see chapter 4)
Sweet-and-sour mix
Tomato juice
Tonic water
Worcestershire sauce

Shopping Wisely

Building a relationship with the right liquor store can prove
invaluable to your drink-making experience.

When I began my cocktail investigations, I went into a
chic spirits store in the heart of Chicago's Gold Coast, which
is the city's swankiest neighborhood. You'd think it was
Tiffany's and the bottles were jewels. The salesmen hovered
over their merchandise, eyeing me as an interloper. It was
not a pleasant experience, nor was it ever repeated.

Nevertheless, I was determined to find retail help. Fortunately it was available at my nearby strip mall. For the store's
owner, who had served thousands of twenty-something
shoppers, no question was too dumb. It was impossible to be
embarrassed talking to him.

He graciously translated garbled requests into clear English.

"What's the stuff with the gold flecks in it?" I would mumble.

"Oh, Goldschlager," he'd reply and go to the back room for an open bottle to sample.

When I reached for a bottle of very expensive apple brandy, I was talked into a more economically priced alternative. Naturally this man hoped to hook a steady customer, and he did.

It may take a little shopping around to find your guardian angel of spirits, but it's worth the search. You may find the perfect match in a chain store or an independent store.

Look for a clean and orderly shop. If bottles are dust-covered, turnover is low. Move on. Also check for organization. You'll want to browse the shelves yourself. Having all the rums in one place and all the liqueurs grouped together, for example, will make your shopping experience easier.

Does the inventory include liquors that are just being introduced in bars and magazine ads? If you want to make fashionable cocktails, you need a store that sells trendy liquors.

The help shouldn't be intrusive, but available.

Don't let someone talk you into buying something because it's on sale. It could be cheap because there's too much of it in the back room and the management is trying to clear it out. Likewise a good salesman won't steer you to the pricey bottles. He or she will ask what you're making and what your budget is before giving suggestions in several price ranges.

Don't stick around for a condescending salesperson. So what if you can't pronounce "slivovitz" (SLIV-uh-vitz). You're a customer and you're eager to learn.

A good liquor store also offers recipe cards, tastings, and demonstrations. You can pick up so much information it's like having a crash course in drink making.

Let's Twist Again

To make lemon twists, cut a lemon lengthwise into six wedges. Pull the fruit away from the peel. Squeeze the fruit for lemon juice. You can keep the juice in a tightly closed container in the refrigerator for several days. Using a paring knife, slice each wedge of rind into long strips, ¼-inch wide. You can make lemon twists several days in advance. Wrap in plastic wrap and refrigerate to store.

The Essential Garnishes

Garnishes decorate a drink, provide flavor, and define the cocktail's essential character. Take a mix of gin and dry vermouth. Add olives and you have a Martini; add cocktail onions instead and you've got a Gibson. It's the garnish that distinguishes the drink.

The maraschino cherry is a key ingredient in a Whiskey Sour or an Old-Fashioned. And even if you're not going to munch on the fruit, you can practice knotting the cherry stem with your tongue. Sorry, but this author hasn't mastered the trick.

When stocking your bar, start with the following basic garnishes:

Pimiento-stuffed olives, large to jumbo
Cocktail onions
Fresh lemons and limes
Maraschino cherries

The Essential Sweeteners

Regular granulated sugar is slow to dissolve in a drink. It leaves an unappealing residue. Instead, you may use bar sugar or superfine sugar, both of which have fine granules and dissolve faster. You can also make a simple syrup to sweeten drinks (see chapter 4 for recipe).

Bar sugar or superfine sugar
Simple syrup

The Essential Salts

By now you may be wondering whether you picked up a cookbook or a drink book. Be assured, this is the last word (for now) on kitchen ingredients. Don't rim a glass with table salt. It's too fine grained. Instead, use one of the following:

Margarita salt, available in liquor or specialty food stores
Sea salt, available in specialty food stores

Ice Talk

You're using fresh, homemade mixers and the best-quality liquor you can afford. Don't ruin things by using ice cubes that have been sitting in the freezer for weeks, absorbing odors. Imagine putting an ice cube that reeks of garlic into a Gin Gimlet. Not an experience you'll treasure.

The downside of modern refrigerator units with automatic ice makers is that you may be tempted to use ice that's cloudy and tainted with flavor impurities, ice that doesn't start with distilled water. Save freezer ice for your own soft drinks.

Take the extra step and buy a bag of ice cubes for a party. When you're serving yourself a before-dinner cocktail, use ice cubes you've recently made. Toss out ice cubes that have been lingering in the freezer more than a couple of days. You'll taste the difference fresh ice makes.

Use ice cubes for highballs and for on-the-rocks drinks. Use cracked ice for shaken or blender drinks. Or buy crushed ice for blender drinks.

Clear As Ice

Research scientists at Argonne National Laboratories in Batavia, Illinois, who are usually involved in experiments designed for the country's well-being, come to the rescue here as well, offering their recipe for clear ice cubes:

First pour tap water into a pot. Then bring it to a boil for at least 5 minutes. Cool to near room temperature in the pot. Next pour the water into ice-cube trays being careful to not disturb or stir up the water any more than necessary. Place the tray in the freezer until solid.

Dissolved gases often cause clear liquids to turn opaque when frozen, say the scientists.

 ## THE QUALITY QUESTION

You instinctively want to serve your guests the very best brands of alcohol you can afford. And why not? You wouldn't want to spoil the flavor of a drink you've so carefully crafted with a raw-tasting alcohol, nor do you want to give your guests the impression of being miserly. But being price-blind isn't always beneficial. Instead, match your liquors to the event and the specific drink.

For example, if you're making Rum Punch for twenty-five at your backyard barbecue, put away the aged rum you brought back from Jamaica. You want to quench thirsts, and whatever rum your local store is featuring will do the trick.

Likewise, forego the premium products when you're making a fruity drink in which the flavoring agents will blunt the taste of the alcohol. Why use a fine product when you're shaking it up with coconut cream and pureed bananas?

Use the highest quality when you're serving liquor straight-up, on the rocks, or with soda. Serve products you're proud of when you're entertaining friends who appreciate the taste.

As an aside, price isn't necessarily a reflection of finesse. A good percentage of your bottle's cost goes into packaging and advertising. Companies spend more than $272 million a year to advertise distilled spirits alone. (And that's a drop in the bottle compared to the $722 million spent on beer advertising.)

Don't judge a spirit by its price tag; judge by its taste, aroma, and clarity. Whenever you order a drink in a bar, restaurant, or someone's home, make a note when you come across a liquor you like. Buy the product that tastes good to you.

Mixers, however, are another matter. Buy the best tonic water, club soda, and soft drinks. The price difference is just a matter of pennies. Be sure to use fresh fruit for blended drinks; canned or bottled flavorings have an artificial taste that won't enhance your drink.

Now that you're familiar with spirits and mixers, clear a shelf in your cupboard or set up your bar cart. Stock up on the bottles that reflect your taste preferences. You'll learn how to satisfy your cocktail cravings in upcoming chapters.

3

Toys and More

Bartending Utensils, Gadgets, and Gizmos

What's in the glass is only the beginning. The right tools and glassware are themselves part of the drink ritual. Each glass shape is associated with a particular drink. For example, the V-shaped cocktail glass is perfect for a Martini. The design has risen above glassware to become an icon for sophistication. Just look at a cocktail glass. It says "style," doesn't it? And how could you serve a frothy Piña Colada in anything but the shapely piña colada glass, sculpted like a top-heavy hourglass? You'll find that using the correct glass enhances your drink experience. This chapter describes the standard glassware and the drinks for each. Once you're comfortably stocked with the basics, you may want to branch out to more distinctive glasses. Check the Resources section at the end of the book for stores that sell designer glasses.

Bartending is easier and more pleasurable if you've got the right tools. They don't have to be expensive; some of the basics may already be in your kitchen. As you progress in your bartending skills, you'll find that some simple and inexpensive gadgets can be extremely helpful—letting you flick the zest from your lemon, muddle your mint, or spear your orange slices with elegant flair. When your hobby becomes a passion, check out the bigger and more esoteric toys—ice shavers, bar trolleys, and caddies that enhance your mixology magic.

These ideas are intended to launch you on the delights of drink making. You're free to adapt the lists to your needs.

Helpful Hint

If you're asked to "build" a cocktail, you'll add ice to a glass, and then pour all the ingredients into the glass in the order specified. Don't use a shaker.

 ## THE GLASS CLASS

You'll find glassware in so many styles and in so many price ranges, you can choose enough to fill every cupboard space. Your parents probably bought sets of glasses and the design of the highball glasses matched that of the cocktail glasses. Don't worry about this. Don't concern yourself that every margarita glass be part of a matched set. In fact, an eclectic glassware collection will be distinctive and useful. Guests won't have to ask which is their glass. And you won't be so concerned if one glass breaks.

Concentrate your efforts on selecting glasses suited to the drinks you're most likely to serve. Through a combination of tradition, folklore, and design, certain glasses have come to be associated with specific drinks. Although you could serve a Martini in a jelly

---

Fun Fact!

When a bartender says he's "breaking a bottle," don't duck for flying glass. The term "break" means to empty a bottle. Laws used to require bartenders to break all empty liquor bottles when the bar closed for the night.

Beginner's Glass Collection

The absolute beginner's glass collection should include four to six each of the following:

Cocktail

Highball

Shot

glass, you'll want to show off its shimmering, cool good looks with the classic V-shaped cocktail glass, for example.

Use the absolute beginner's list for starters, buying four to six of each shape, more if you entertain crowds. Then add to your collection. Here are some of the most popular glasses along with the drinks they're associated with.

Beer mug: A thick glass that can be chilled to keep beverages cold. It has a handle for easy holding and will be deep enough to hold 12 ounces of beer plus a 1-inch head of foam.

Brandy snifter: A balloon-shaped bowl that narrows slightly at the rim. The sizes vary greatly and the glass can hold anywhere from 3 to 25 ounces. In this author's opinion, 25-ounce snifters should be used as goldfish bowls. Go for the 3- to 10-ounce size and don't fill more than ¼ full, or 1½ ounces.

Cocktail: A V-shaped glass on a tall stem. This is the classic martini glass. Its capacity ranges from 3 to 10 ounces. Purists insist the glass be clear, so you can see your drink, but in the 1920s, New York's fashionable Algonquin Hotel served Martinis in blue glasses. You'll also want to use a cocktail glass for Gin Gimlets. Oversized versions of the cocktail glass can be used for Margaritas.

The Best Champagne Glass

Historians debate whether the saucer-shaped champagne glass is actually based on the shape of Marie Antoinette's breast. There's research suggesting she ordered a Parisian manufacturer to make glasses from an imprint of her breast. Experts do agree that the flat shape isn't suited to champagne. It allows the bubbles to be released too quickly. Save the saucers for dessert; use flutes for sparkling wines.

Collins: A tall, straight, narrow glass that holds at least 10 ounces of liquid. Use this for a Tom Collins or a glass of club soda with a lime wedge.

Cordial: A little stemmed glass you can fill with 1 to 2 ounces of sherry or a liqueur.

Flute: A long, tapering glass with a long stem, also called a champagne glass. Most flutes can be filled with 4 to 6 ounces of the bubbly. Don't fill a flute to the very top with champagne, however. You want the bubbles to dance inside the glass.

Highball: A tall glass, similar to a collins glass, but slightly wider and less delicate looking, holding about 8 to 10 ounces. This is an all-purpose glass for tall drinks such as a Gin and Tonic or a Bloody Mary.

Margarita: Similar to a cocktail glass, but curved, not angular, with a 10-ounce capacity. Serve Margaritas or Daiquiris in this glass.

Old-Fashioned: A sturdy, straight glass that holds about 8 ounces of liquid. In addition to holding an Old-Fashioned, this glass is suitable for a Manhattan, Bullshot, Rob Roy, or Rusty Nail.

Piña Colada: A stemmed glass that is round on the bottom, slightly tapered in the center, and flared out again at the lip. It holds at least 8 ounces.

Pousse-Café: An elegant, small, straight-sided glass with a stem. The design makes it easier to pour in layers of liquor. Use these to try your hand at a Cherry-Orange Delight or Chocolate Cream Cherry.

Shot: A small, squarish glass that fits in the fist of your hand and holds about 1½ ounces of liquid. Use it for a neat drink, such as a shot of whiskey.

> **Fun Fact!**
> Tell your guest you're pouring her drink into a bucket and watch her blanch. You'll relieve her by explaining that a bucket is an old-fashioned glass.

Sour (or whiskey sour): A stemmed glass that resembles a miniature wine glass. The bowl-shaped glass has a 5-ounce capacity and is used for Whiskey Sours.

Wine: A long, curved bowl on a stem. Wine glasses come in several sizes, each designed to hold a specific type of wine. You can limit yourself to a white wine glass that holds about 8 ounces or choose the larger red wine glass that will take 12 ounces or more.

Ensuring Spotless Glasses

As the home bartender you'll discover that streaks, spots, and evaporation marks on glassware are irritating and embarrassing. You want to concentrate your efforts on making a fabulous cocktail, not disguising the blotches on the glass.

You can avoid this party-time anxiety by using the proper techniques to wash and store your glasses. Don't put glass washing off until the last minute. Clean your glassware when the party is over. If it's been a long time since your last bash and your glassware is dusty, clean it a day in advance.

First, use a diluted dishwashing liquid and hand wash in hot water. Follow with a thorough rinse in cold water. If you insist on using your dishwasher, hand rinse your glasses before adding to the machine. When the cycle is finished, inspect all the glasses. If you have stubborn water spots, fill a large bowl with cold water and the juice of one lemon. Dunk the glasses in the lemon water after rinsing.

Dry the glasses on a rack over a draining board. Then go over each glass with a lint-free towel. Store glasses right-side up in your cupboard. Upside-down glasses can develop a musty odor. If you do this when your party is over, you'll be able to reach for clean, spot-free glassware the next time guests drop by.

LITTLE TOYS

Just as you'd use a teaspoon and not a soup spoon to get the correct proportion of baking powder for a cake, you'll want to use the right tool to assure a great drink. Start with the essentials and add on as you become more experimental.

Now that the cocktail hour is back, you'll find that lifestyle stores (such as Crate & Barrel, Williams-Sonoma, or Restoration Hardware) carry an array of shakers, knives, bottle openers, and other accessories. You may also shop in restaurant-supply houses. The designs may not be as elegant, but the prices are lower than in a lot of consumer stores.

Here are some suggestions for bar equipment.

Bar spoons: Long-handled spoons designed for stirring drinks. Make sure the spoon is narrow enough to get to the bottom of any glass. Choose one spoon that has a twisted handle. This is more than decorative. Trickle a spirit down the spiral spoon handle and you'll master the Pousse-Café (see chapter 5 for details). You'll want one spiral spoon and one or two straight-sided spoons.

Bottle- and can opener: Get the best quality you can find. Skip the electric can openers; they take up a lot of space and aren't very portable.

Corkscrew: The fold-up type called a "waiter's friend" is small, economical, and easy to use, though you may find that a wing opener, in which the handles act as levers, is fail-proof.

Cutting board: A good-quality wood or heavy plastic board will save valuable surfaces as you slice up lemons and other garnishes. A small 5- by 7-inch board is all you need.

Ice bucket: This is an essential part of a well-stocked bar, so choose wisely. Find a bucket large enough to hold at least 1 quart of ice cubes. A larger size may not be practical because it takes up a lot of counter space. In addition, you should keep some ice cubes in reserve in the freezer. You'll see glass, plastic, and stainless steel ice buckets. Stainless steel does a good job of preventing ice from melting. If you invest in an expensive model, look for a drainage cup in the bottom to gather water. And don't forget the tongs.

Jigger: A finger-sized measuring cup. Jiggers either come in a single measure, such as the 1½-ounce size that defines the jigger, or with marked gradations ranging up to 3 ounces. Choose the latter if you can find it. You'll avoid having to buy an assortment of jiggers. A jigger is also a little glass used to serve a shot of liquor, about 1½ ounces worth.

Juicer: The old-fashioned ridged oval set over a straining bowl works well. Look for a juicer set over a measuring cup. This type allows you to know as soon as you've got enough juice for your drink.

Knives: Buy a serrated knife for slicing lemons and limes and a paring knife for making lemon curls. You may find that wooden-handled knives are easier to grasp if your hands are wet from handling ice and mixers.

Measuring spoons: Jiggers don't get down to teaspoons (and some jiggers don't measure a tablespoon, which is ½ ounce), so you'll want a set of measuring spoons. I prefer spoons attached together with a ring so I don't lose one.

Muddler: A spoon with a flat, wooden bowl that allows you to crush herbs into a drink without scratching the glass. One is all you need unless you intend to have a Mint Julep party to celebrate the Kentucky Derby.

Pitcher: If you enjoy Sangria, fruit punches, or Mulled Wine, you'll want a pitcher to serve drinks. Choose a design that holds at least a quart of liquid, but make sure the pitcher is heat and cold resistant.

Shaker: Read enough cocktail books or check enough Web sites and you'll see more descriptions of this two- or three-piece gadget than you can shake a Whiskey Sour at. A shaker is the tool that distinguishes a cocktail creation from a mere drink. It's essential for mixing and rapidly chilling drinks. Add ice, liquor, and mixer. Shake for a minute, or until your hands cry mercy and you're ready to strain an icy drink into a glass. You'll see many wonderful, fun, and tempting designs such as penguins or art deco trains. However, shakers fall into two basic categories. One is a set containing a mixing glass with printed-on measurement indicators and a stainless steel cone of the same size that fits upside-down over the glass. This is called a Boston or American shaker. If you choose this variety, you'll need to strain your cocktail using an additional piece of equipment. The second type is a three-piece unit including a tumbler, cap, and built-in strainer. It's referred to as a Manhattan or European shaker. You'll find shakers in a variety of shapes and sizes. Web sites are dedicated to collectible shakers. Choose the shape and size that fit your entertaining style, or buy two. Small shakers are uncommon, which is a pity since they're so useful. An 8- to 10-ounce shaker is marvelous when you're making a drink for yourself. Larger sizes, such 14-, 16-, or 24-ounce shakers, are essential for parties because you can mix a batch of cocktails in one shake.

Speed pourer: A plastic spout that fits over a bottle opening, allowing you to pour beverages without dribbling.

Stirring rod: Like shakers, stirring rods can be as silly or as practical as you'd like. A rod is useful for stirring tall drinks or drinks by the pitcherful. A simple metal version is fine for this. Then, if you want, select some fun or fancy designs to grace your bar.

Strainer: Even if your shaker has a strainer, you'll need something to hold back the ice in stirred drinks. A little coil-rimmed Hawthorne strainer works well.

Tongs: If you ever try to scoop ice cubes from a bucket using a soup spoon, you'll quickly see the merits of a good pair of tongs. Find tongs with insulated rubber grip handles if possible. They don't get as cold and are easy to handle if you've got a lot of ice to serve.

Towels: Choose two or three white linen towels for wiping glassware and your hands.

Tray: You don't have to look like Jeeves. Trays come in a marvelous range of sizes and materials. Your best bet is whatever you feel comfortable carrying. Select a tray with a lip, so any spilled liquids will be contained. Also, choose a tray with an easy-to-clean surface such as plastic, stainless steel, or treated wood.

Tumbler: A tall, stainless steel container, resembling those old-fashioned malted milk tumblers, is just what you need to stir, not shake, a couple of drinks at a time. Your tumbler should hold at least 16 ounces.

Zester: A handheld tool for scraping the fine outer peel from a lemon, orange, or lime. You'll find this is faster and easier to use than a paring knife, though not as versatile. Again, shop for a rubber-handled utensil that's easy to grip.

BIG TOYS

As a bartender, you'll want some accessories that make your job easier and more enjoyable. Having a turbo-charged ice grinder or musical drink cart (I'm making this up. I've never seen a cart that plays bar music . . . yet) is a convenience and a kick. And yes, even as an adult, you get to have fun with toys; this time it's bar toys.

Here are some bar tools to play with:

Bar caddy: You're probably not going to bring your guests into the kitchen, but you can bring the best of the kitchen to your entertaining area with a bar caddy. One deluxe package includes a three-cubic-foot refrigerator with lights so you can see the contents inside, an ice chest, and a Corian bar top. The caddy is on wheels, so you can store it when not in use. You'll find it in professional bar supply houses and on the Web (see Resources) for about $3,800 to $4,000.

Oh, yes, and if you want to spend about $6,400 you can upgrade to a caddy that has automatic defrost and space for a half keg of beer.

Blender: This isn't an option for a cocktail host. Some books recommend an ice bag and a mallet. That's about as helpful as using a sheaf of wheat to make a whiskey on the rocks. You need a blender. Period. You have to decide what bells and whistles it should have. This appliance can do several things: mince, puree, blend, aerate, and frappé. You'll want a model that can crush ice. You can buy an all-purpose blender to handle all your chores, or buy a specifically designed bar blender. Expect to pay at least $50 for a good-quality kitchen blender and twice that for a bar appliance.

If tailgating is one of your passions, check out the blenders that plug into your car's cigarette lighter and retail for about $100. Piña Coladas at halftime anyone?

Ice crusher: An old-fashioned hand-crank gadget. It will run you about $40 and grinds a quart of ice in two minutes. That's quicker than a run to the convenience store.

Martini mister: Imagine being in a jungle, 100 miles from the closest bar. You've got a bottle of gin in your backpack, but you can't swig gin. After all, you're a civilized drinker.

Then you realize you've packed your trusty Martini mister, a handy 1-ounce spray container you've filled with dry vermouth. Ah, life is worth living again. This is what I consider a silly toy, but a fun conversation piece. You'll find a Martini mister in better spirits stores.

Snow cone maker: Remember those frosty cones of shaved ice topped with blue sugar syrup? They stained your lips as they chilled your insides. Snow cone makers are back. But now you've got more inventive ways to use these gadgets. How about a Mai Tai snow cone?

Choose from two versions of this utensil.

First, there's a hand-crank model that sells for less than $20. Arrange a block of frozen liquid, such as that Mai Tai (as an aside, alcoholic mixtures take longer to freeze and may never be as solid as water), into the insulated container. Turn the handle and produce flavored "snow."

The second type is called an Electric Hawaiice Shaver and costs about $60. No handle to turn; the machine creates shaved ice that you flavor with syrup. Pour a Mint Julep or Cosmopolitan over shaved ice and enjoy an instant vacation.

Trolley: A mobile unit with counter space and shelving, which may offer the space you need for your party-giving supplies. A trolley is an excellent investment. It's essential if you live in a cramped studio apartment. In fact, you'll find it so useful you may want to buy an extra for everyday storage. Look for a multi-tiered unit with a water-resistant surface, glass racks, wine racks, and space for bottles. (I found a trolley at Crate & Barrel several years ago. It's 38 inches tall and has two rows of wine racks and one shelf for bottles. When I'm not bartending, I store old newspapers and phone books in the space.)

Assembling your bar equipment isn't a matter of buying the most expensive and flashy toys. Heck, the Screwdriver was supposedly named when someone stirred together orange juice and vodka, using the trusty tool. When you do shop, look for utensils that save you time, improve your drink-making skills, and fit your space. If you don't have the budget for everything on your list, browse secondhand shops or garage sales. You may find glassware, tumblers, and spoons that are well-crafted and inexpensive.

So, You Want to
Make a Cocktail?

A Step-by-Step Guide
to Making Classic Drinks

S can a few drink compendiums and you'll be struck by
the number of spirit combinations mixologists create.
You could make 100 different vodka cocktails—such as
Polynesian pepper pot, or prairie oyster, or copper head—
without repeating one.

Where do you start?

At the beginning, of course.

You bought this book to learn the absolute basics. And, in
drinks, as in anything else, you'll learn the building blocks
before you move on. You're not going to make crepes before
you master pancakes, so why challenge yourself to a multilayered Pousse-Café before you've poured your first Martini?

Many of your favorite drinks, such as Champagne Cocktails, Black Russians, and Sidecars, were created decades
ago. A Sidecar, for example, is a post-World War I invention;
the Black Russian was invented during the Cold War.

That's not to say things shouldn't change. (In chapter 5, you'll see plenty of new cocktail recipes.) But a sip of one of the classic recipes that follow is proof that a well-designed cocktail is ageless. *The Absolute Beginner's* drink recipes were researched through several decades of bartending guides. Recipes were tested and retested so the results are both tasty and true to the original drink.

SIMPLE SYRUP

Many of the following recipes call for Simple Syrup, a sugar-and-water solution you'll use to sweeten many drinks. It's important to learn the basics of making it before you proceed.

SIMPLE SYRUP

When it comes to Simple Syrup, most recipes call for a proportion of two parts sugar to one part water. That yields a syrup that's extremely sweet and sticky and tends to clump up when mixed with ice.

The following recipe is a change from the usual directions. It calls for one-and-a-half parts sugar to one part water. You'll find that it's easy to make, doesn't get too thick, and works well in sweet-and-sour drinks. The one-and-a-half-to-one formula was used for this book's cocktails.

1½ cups sugar

1   cup water

In a small pot, combine sugar and water. Bring to a boil over medium heat. Reduce to low and cook until sugar completely dissolves, about 10 minutes. Do not stir or sugar clumps will form. Remove from heat. Cool to room temperature. Pour into an attractive container, cover tightly, and refrigerate. This will keep several weeks.

Makes 2½ cups.

LITE SIMPLE SYRUP

A tablespoon of sugar has almost 50 calories. If you eliminate half a cup of sugar you'll save 400 calories on the total recipe.

1   cup sugar

1   cup water

In a small pot, combine sugar and water. Bring to a boil over medium heat. Reduce to low and cook until sugar completely dissolves, about 10 minutes. Do not stir or sugar clumps will form. Remove from heat. Cool to room temperature. Pour into an attractive container, cover tightly, and refrigerate. This will keep several weeks.

Makes 1½ cups.

DRINKS: THE THREE BASIC CATEGORIES

First, let's demystify those drink choices. Of the hundreds, even thousands of drink options, you'll basically deal with three categories: the highball, the lowball, and the shaken cocktail.

Highballs are all the drinks poured into tall ice-filled glasses. The possibilities range from Scotch and soda to a Tom Collins. Lowballs are stirred cocktails, such as Cosmopolitans or Manhattans. Shaken drinks cover anything you'd put in a shaker and do a little dance to, including a Margarita. You could add another category for

> **Fun Fact!**
>
> The word "highball," a combination of spirits and mixer, was originally a railroad term. The signalman raised a ball on a pole to get the motorman to speed up. Synonyms for highball include "get a move on," or "hotfoot it."

blender drinks, such as a Frozen Raspberry Daiquiri, or call these extremely shaken.

MAKING THE PERFECT DRINK

First and foremost, it's essential to add ingredients in the proper order. Ice must always be first. It's a painful lesson I was taught as a young kitten. The older-man object of my attention was invited in for a Gin and Tonic, and I, being green, proceeded to pour some gin and tonic into a glass and top the mixture with a handful of ice cubes. Never was a cocktail met with such scorn. Tossed out, melting ice and all, and with it an unrequited romance.

> ### Helpful Hint
>
> You'll notice that the recipes require you to pour alcohol over ice in a glass. The ice comes first so it chills the glass and the spirits to follow.

That, dear reader, is why you should never underestimate the power of a well-made drink, or the potential damage of a poorly made one.

And that's why you'll want to master preparation techniques for the three (or four, if you prefer) drink styles. *The Absolute Beginner's Guide* won't let you down. You'll read all you need to know.

If you're not ready to risk romance or your reputation on individual cocktails, pitcher drinks—stirred drinks in quantity—are an easy alternative, especially if you're serving a crowd.

You can choose your recipe according to a theme: Southwestern, Caribbean, or Old English, for example. Make your drinks appropriate to the season: Mulled Wine in December, Sangria in July.

Unfortunately, some hosts think pitcher drinks offer an opportunity to cut corners. Not in this book. You'll pick up valuable tips on how to make excellent quality cocktails by the pitcherful.

And despite the alcoholic choices, there will be times when you want a sophisticated drink without liquor—something lively and original with more flair than a soft drink. Chapter 6 provides alcohol-free and low-alcohol recipes along with suggestions for making these drinks as exciting as the more spirited versions.

 ## POURING, MEASURING, AND MIXING

The bartender's graceful movements while pouring a perfect measure of whiskey into an old-fashioned glass are enviable. Do people go to school to learn drink choreography? Picture it: Twenty bartenders line up, lift bottle, tilt, and pour. Dribble any and go to the back of the class.

Pouring a drink takes some skill. But you don't need a bartending degree. With a little practice you'll have confidence as you fill every glass, even if you have a line of ten thirsty guests waiting for their drinks.

As you start, you'll rely on measuring spoons and jiggers to accurately reproduce the drinks in this book. But once you become more proficient, you'll want to get rid of the bar equivalent of training wheels.

In this chapter, you'll learn bartenders' tricks for getting proportioned drinks without using measurements. However, even after you've gained some experience, use your tools whenever you're making a batch of drinks or mixing a new cocktail. It's the only way you'll be assured of a drink that has an appealing balance of flavor and alcohol. A good-tasting drink is not based on guesswork.

> **Helpful Hint**
>
> Wipe the rims of liquor bottles before you close them up for the night. Any sticky liquid will make it harder to open the bottle next time.

From High to Low

To pour a highball, such as a Screwdriver or Gin and Tonic, fill a highball glass two-thirds full of ice. Always add ice first so the glass is cold and the liquor chills quickly. Next add the liquor. Then pour in the mixer, leaving a half inch of space to prevent spilling. Stir a nonbubbly drink well to mix it; stir a carbonated cocktail once or twice. Finally, add the garnish.

Lowballs, which include stirred drinks, offer a couple of possibilities.

For an on-the-rocks drink, fill a lowball glass half full with ice. Add the liquor, then the mixer, and stir. For a chilled drink without the ice, such as a Martini, fill a tumbler two-thirds full with ice. Add the liquor, then the mixer, stir and strain into the lowball glass.

Bartender Tricks: Let It Flow, Let It Flow, Let It Flow

Get a firm grip on the bottle. With one smooth movement, tip the bottle into a jigger or into a glass. Don't jerk the bottle up to see what you're doing. When you've poured the proper amount, give the bottle a quarter turn to stop the flow and bring the bottle upright in one motion. That's the end of dribbles.

After a few drinks or a few parties, you'll want to try a freehand style. Employ some bartender tricks.

- For a short drink, wrap your index and middle finger around the glass. Pour liquor to the top of your fingers, which is roughly one jigger or $1\frac{1}{2}$ ounces.
- Use a speed pourer. Attach the special spout to your bottle. Fill the glass with ice, then flip the liquor bottle upside down over the glass and silently count to three as you pour. Turn the bottle right-side up. You should be dispensing $1\frac{1}{2}$ to 2 ounces of liquor.
- When you're pouring several servings of the same drink at one time, line up your glasses. Fill each halfway, then pour again so all the glasses are filled evenly.

Let It Pour

Pouring liquids is a skill you probably mastered in preschool. Thank goodness you don't spill Kool-Aid all over the kitchen counter anymore. Still, whenever you pour a drink for a guest it's a challenge to get a little liquor into a glass. It's not you. Pouring party drinks can be stressful. At times, you're facing six or more thirsty guests and handling wet, slippery glasses.

Take your time. Let your guests know their patience will be rewarded by your good judgment and expertise.

Do use a jigger when you're first making drinks. You'll build confidence as you pour the proper measure. Fill the jigger accordingly, and pour from the jigger into the glass.

- Never fill a drink higher than ½ inch from the rim of the glass. Allow enough room so that the addition of garnishes won't cause the drink to overflow.
- Fill wine glasses ⅓ to ½ full so the wine's aromas can be released into the glass, not the air. Fill brandy snifters with no more than 1½ ounces of brandy.

Stirring Tales

Mixing a cocktail without disturbing the bubbles or clarity of the drink requires the most minimal of stirring skills. If you've got a stirring rod and a flexible wrist, you're set.

Pour your drink ingredients into a glass filled with the appropriate amount of ice. For a still mixture, stir gently but well. For a carbonated mixture, stir only once or twice so you don't disturb the bubbles.

When making a pitcher drink that requires ice, combine the alcohol and flavorings in a tumbler. Pour the mixture into a pitcher chilled with added ice, then add any carbonated beverages and stir once or twice. Some pitcher drinks, such as Black Velvet, don't need ice. The liquids are cold enough.

Blender Tricks

Did you know blenders can dance? Ignore a blender while it's grinding ice and it will rock its way off the counter to crash on the floor.

Did you know that blenders can have hissy fits, spewing pureed food all over your walls? Too true. It happens and this author will tell you that Frozen Raspberry Daiquiri-stained silk is not a fashion statement.

Blenders have powerful motors. That's why you have one. And that's why you should pay attention when you use the appliance.

Gather all your ingredients before you start so you're not tempted to walk halfway across your apartment for more ice while your machine is running. Add each item in the order directed in your recipe. Always add the cover and the pouring cap before you turn your blender on. Do not lift the lid when the machine is churning. And don't try to dislodge a stuck ingredient with a spoon or a spatula and especially not with your finger while the blender is running. If your machine is noisy, set it on top of a towel, which will absorb some of the rumblings.

> **Helpful Hint**
>
> A word about cleaning up. Keep a damp cloth and a couple of dry towels on hand when you're mixing drinks in order to clean up as you go. A wet and sticky work area is more likely to cause accidents.

To make blender drinks, first pour in the liquor, then the mixer, and then the ice, filling the container half full for several drinks. Use four or five ice cubes for each drink (one serving). Or you can try crushed ice so that your blender won't have to work as hard. Use 1 cup of crushed ice per drink. Firmly cover the blender container with the lid. Start at slow speed for thirty seconds to coarsely crush the ice, then switch to high speed. When

Chilling Out

Your drink will stay colder if you pour it into a chilled glass. To do so:

- Fill the glass with ice, swirl it around for a couple of minutes, then discard the ice and proceed immediately to make the drink.
- Store glasses in the refrigerator to save time.
- To frost a glass, dip it in cold water, then place in the freezer up to three hours.

Store mixers in the refrigerator to keep drinks colder. And always provide plenty of napkins with chilled glasses.

you no longer hear ice chips breaking up and the mixture looks frothy, turn off the machine. Pour the drink into chilled glasses.

Whole Lotta Shaking Going On

Shake if you want an ice-cold drink and don't mind that it isn't crystal clear. Fill your shaker about half full with ice. A loosely packed shaker will assure that liquids have space to dance around the ice cubes. Then add the liquor and any flavoring or mixers. Don't add carbonated beverages to a shaker unless you want to take all the bubbles out of your drink. Cap the shaker and give your arms a workout. Open your shaker when it's as frosty as Wisconsin in January.

You may notice the shaker seems impossible to open. You didn't goof. The combination of liquid, ice, and physics causes the parts to form a seal. Gently tap the seam of the two shaker pieces and they'll loosen.

Strain your drink into a glass using the built-in shaker strainer or a coil-rimmed strainer.

Measuring

You're familiar with most of the measuring terms used for drinks. Teaspoons and tablespoons are the same amounts you'd use in cooking. But did you know a pony isn't a braying animal, but a 1-ounce measure? Or how about a jigger? It's not a skin-borrowing tick but a 1½-ounce serving or a glass that holds a small amount of liquid. In addition it's a measuring implement. You'll want to know these measurements so you can create drinks that are balanced in flavor and in alcohol. Refer to the "Measure by Measure" chart below for information on exact quantities.

> **Fun Fact!**
>
> French Champagne maker Pol Roger created a 20-fluid-ounce bottle specifically for Winston Churchill. His man-servant brought him a bottle every morning.

Measure by Measure

1 drop	⅟₃₂ teaspoon
2 drops	⅟₁₆ teaspoon
1 teaspoon	⅓ tablespoon or ⅙ ounce
½ tablespoon	1½ teaspoons or ¼ ounce
1 tablespoon	3 teaspoons or ½ ounce
2 tablespoons	⅛ cup or 1 ounce
Pony	2 tablespoons, ⅛ cup, or 1 ounce
Jigger	3 tablespoons or 1½ ounces
¼ cup	4 tablespoons or 2 ounces
½ cup	8 tablespoons or 4 ounces
1 cup	16 tablespoons or 8 ounces

Although you probably still buy milk in the standard 32-ounce quart size, most liquor and wine companies sell their products in metric-size bottles. It can get confusing if you're expecting an 8-ounce half-pint, but instead get 6.8 ounces. The "By the Bottle" chart on the next page should clear the air, or at least the measuring cup.

By the Bottle

LIQUOR BOTTLES

Standard measure

Pint	16 ounces
Fifth	25.6 ounces
Quart	32 ounces

Metric measure

500 milliliters	16.9 ounces
750 milliliters	25.4 ounces
1 liter	33.8 ounces

BY THE WINE BOTTLE

Split	6.3 ounces or 187 milliliters
Tenth	12.7 ounces or 375 milliliters
Fifth	25.4 ounces or 750 milliliters

BY THE CHAMPAGNE BOTTLE
(AND THIS GETS ABSOLUTELY BIBLICAL)

Magnum	50.7 ounces or 1.5 liters
Jeroboam	101.4 ounces or 3 liters
Rehaboam	152 ounces or 4.5 liters
Methuselah	203 ounces or 6 liters

THE CLASSICS: DRINK RECIPES

The following recipes are tried and true. Drinks are organized in alphabetical order.

Fun Fact!

Rehaboam was King Solomon's son, who reigned after his death; Methuselah is a biblical character who lived to the ripe age of 969. Did the six-liter bottle of champagne aid his longevity?

BACARDI

If you live in New York State, you must use Bacardi brand rum to make a Bacardi cocktail according to a 1930s state supreme court ruling.

Ice cubes

1½ ounces (3 tablespoons) light rum

½ ounce (1 tablespoon) lime juice

2 teaspoons grenadine

1 maraschino cherry

Fill a shaker half full with ice. Add rum, lime juice, and grenadine and shake well. Strain into cocktail glass. Run a plastic toothpick or short plastic skewer through the cherry and lay across the top of the glass.

Serves 1.

BLACK RUSSIAN

This after-dinner drink dates back to the 1950s. Although American-Soviet relations were politically strained at the time, that didn't prevent American bartenders from naming drinks after Russians.

1½ ounces (3 tablespoons) vodka

¾ ounce (1½ tablespoons) Kahlúa

Pour vodka into an old-fashioned glass. Top with Kahlúa and stir.

Serves 1.

Note: For a White Russian, either float a half-ounce (1 tablespoon) cream on top of the drink after you stir the vodka and Kahlúa together or make a Pousse-Café with three separate layers, starting with the Kahlúa and ending with the cream. See chapter 5 for help with floating drinks.

BLOODY MARY

Fernand Petiot, an American bartender in Paris, mixed equal parts tomato juice and vodka to create the original Bloody Mary, named for the Bucket of Blood Club in Chicago. The formula is getting hotter, with the addition of red pepper sauce and even horseradish in some versions. But no, it's not a hangover cure.

Ice cubes

1½ ounces (3 tablespoons) vodka

4   ounces (½ cup) tomato juice

1   teaspoon lemon juice

½   teaspoon Worcestershire sauce

2   drops hot pepper sauce

⅛   teaspoon celery salt

⅛   teaspoon black pepper

1   celery stalk

Fill a highball glass two-thirds full with ice. Pour in vodka, tomato juice, lemon juice, and Worcestershire sauce. Add hot pepper sauce, celery salt, and pepper. Stir well. Garnish with celery stalk.

Serves 1.

BULLSHOT

Some people opt for this drink the morning after an overindulgence. The thinking is that the protein in the broth is a restorative. Not so! But it is a refreshing brunch cocktail.

Ice cubes

2   ounces (¼ cup) vodka

4   ounces (½ cup) beef broth, chilled

4   drops Worcestershire sauce

2   drops hot red pepper sauce (optional)

Dash of celery salt

1   teaspoon fresh lemon juice

1   lemon wedge

Fill an old-fashioned glass half full with ice. Add vodka, beef broth, Worcestershire sauce, hot pepper sauce (if desired), celery salt, and lemon juice. Stir well. Garnish with lemon wedge.

Serves 1.

CHAMPAGNE COCKTAIL

This sophisticated drink was served in the best New York bars in the late 1800s. There are several versions, including one with a shot of Cognac. If that whets your thirst, add the Cognac with the bitters.

1   sugar cube

1   to 2 drops bitters

4   ounces (½ cup) champagne, chilled

Place sugar in a flute (champagne glass). Add 1 or 2 drops bitters to the sugar cube. Pour on champagne. Serve immediately.

Serves 1.

CUBA LIBRE

This was Ernest Hemingway's drink. One sip and you can imagine you're fishing for the big one off the Cuban coast while the sun reflects off the blue waters. It's enough to build a thirst.

Ice cubes

1½ ounces (3 tablespoons) light rum

Juice of 1 lime

6   ounces (¾ cup) Coca-Cola

1   lime slice

Fill a collins glass two-thirds full with ice. Add rum and lime juice. Stir. Pour in cola. Stir gently once or twice to keep bubbles intact. Add a lime slice as garnish.

Serves 1.

DAIQUIRI

Cuba's indigenous rum, sugarcane, and lime juice have filled glasses in Cuban bars since the turn of the century. During the 1920s and 1930s, the Daiquiri became popular in literary and Hollywood circles.

Ice cubes

2   ounces (¼ cup) light rum

2   teaspoons simple syrup

¾   ounce (1½ tablespoons) fresh lime juice

Fill a shaker half full with ice. Add rum, simple syrup, and lime juice. Cover and shake well. Strain into a margarita or cocktail glass.

Serves 1.

GIBSON

Some people claim a Gibson is a mere Martini that substitutes onions for olives, but purists argue that the change in garnishes makes all the difference in flavor.

Ice cubes

2   **ounces (¼ cup) gin**

½   **teaspoon dry vermouth**

2   **cocktail pearl onions**

Fill a tumbler two-thirds full with ice. Add gin and vermouth. Stir to mix and chill ingredients. Strain into a chilled cocktail glass. Garnish with onions.

Serves 1.

Fun Fact!

The Gibson was created for Charles Dana Gibson, the artist who drew the voluptuous Gibson girls. Some suggest that a Gibson isn't complete unless it sports two onions, to suggest breasts.

GIN AND TONIC

Gin and Tonic—or do you say "Gin-Tonic?"—is a marvelous example of the highball, first mixed in the late 1800s. The original highball consisted of two ingredients: the spirit and the mixer. Both should be the best quality.

Ice cubes

2 ounces (¼ cup) gin

6 ounces (¾ cup) tonic water, chilled

1 lime wedge

Fill a highball glass two-thirds full with ice. Pour in gin. Fill with tonic water. Stir gently once or twice to mix gin into tonic. Garnish edge of glass with lime wedge.

Serves 1.

Note: Substitute vodka for a Vodka and Tonic.

> ## Fun Fact!
>
> Quinine is the substance in tonic water that gives it its distinctive bitter taste. This South American ingredient was famous as a treatment for reducing malarial fevers. No wonder the heroes in jungle movies sip Gin and Tonics.

GIN FIZZ

This cousin of a Tom Collins is shaken, not stirred. Some versions of this drink call for a raw egg white to add more froth. Omit the egg white because it increases the risk of food-borne illness.

Ice cubes

2 ounces (¼ cup) gin

1 ounce (2 tablespoons) lemon juice

1 teaspoon superfine sugar

Club soda

Lemon wedge

> ## Helpful Hint
>
> Responsible and pleasurable: If you goofed when mixing a drink, toss the results and start again. There's no point in squandering your drink quota sipping a bad cocktail.

Fill a shaker half full with ice. Add gin, lemon juice, and sugar. Cover and shake to mix. Strain drink into a collins glass. Fill with club soda. Stir gently once or twice. Add additional ice cubes if desired. Garnish with lemon wedge.

Serves 1.

Note: Try substituting sloe gin for a slightly sweeter drink.

GIN GIMLET

Some bar historians credit this powerful combination of gin and lime juice to the British who are always encouraging their constituents to get more vitamin C. Or it may be named Gimlet because one drink gives you sharp sight.

Ice cubes

2   ounces (¼ cup) gin, chilled

½ to 1 ounce (1 to 2 tablespoons) Rose's lime juice

Lime slice

Fill a tumbler two-thirds full with ice. Add gin and lime juice. Stir briefly. Strain into a cocktail glass. Add a lime slice for garnish.

Serves 1.

Note: ½ ounce lime juice results in a very dry drink. As you add more lime juice, you enhance the sweet-tart flavor.

HARVEY WALLBANGER

No one knows whether or not Harvey ever existed, but during the 1970s, his image as a fun-lovin' surfer guy inspired a major thirst for this Galliano-topped Screwdriver.

Ice cubes

1½ ounces (3 tablespoons) vodka

6 ounces (¾ cup) orange juice

½ ounce (1 tablespoon) Galliano

Fill a collins glass two-thirds full with ice. Add the vodka and orange juice. Stir. Pour on Galliano. Do not stir, but let it float.

Serves 1.

MANHATTAN

Politics may make strange bedfellows, but great cocktails. According to one story, this drink, which originated in New York's Manhattan Club in the late 1800s, was made in honor of Samuel Tilden's victory in the New York governor's race.

Ice cubes

1½ ounces (3 tablespoons) Canadian whisky

½ ounce (1 tablespoon) sweet vermouth

2 drops bitters

1 maraschino cherry

Fill a tumbler two-thirds full with ice. Add whisky, vermouth, and bitters. Stir several times. Strain into a chilled old-fashioned glass. Add a cherry garnish.

Serves 1.

MARGARITA

Thank the late movie actress Marjorie King for inspiring this drink, first concocted in the 1930s. When she claimed tequila was the only spirit she could tolerate, her host mixed the tequila with lime juice. A legendary cocktail was born.

Coarse salt (see note)

Ice cubes

2   ounces (¼ cup) tequila

¾   ounce (1½ tablespoons) Triple Sec

Juice of 1 lime

1   lime wedge

Place about 1 tablespoon coarse salt on a small plate. Wet the rim of a margarita glass. Dip the rim in the salt. Set glass upright and let dry, about 10 minutes.

Fill shaker half full with ice. Pour in tequila, Triple Sec, and lime juice. Cover and shake well. Strain into prepared glass. Add lime wedge.

Serves 1.

Note: For a fruity Margarita, add ¼ cup of your favorite pureed fruit to the shaker with the other ingredients. For a frozen Margarita, add the ingredients, including fruit and ice, to a blender.

MARTINI

You'll read many dicta on the perfect Martini. This is a drink with more possible proportions than the Miss Universe pageant: one part dry vermouth to 6 parts gin; one to 10, or a spritz from a vermouth atomizer. Do you stir, shake, or rumba?

The Quintessential American Cocktail

The Martini is bold, gutsy, straightforward, and very adaptable.

But who was the mixology genius who first concocted a Martini? Several people vie for the title. Some claim the Martini was invented by the bartender of the former Occidental Hotel in San Francisco in the 1860s and named for the nearby town of Martinez. Another version suggests the drink was first made in Martinez itself. East Coast boosters credit the Knickerbocker Hotel in New York City in the early part of the twentieth century.

Despite its longevity (more than 100 years if you believe the stories), the Martini's fortunes come and go. Gin, being easier to concoct than scotch, led to the drink's popularity during Prohibition. And if you ever saw *The Thin Man* movies of the 1930s, you'd know that sophisticated people all sipped one-too-many Martinis.

Martini shakers were put on hold during World War II. But no sooner did young post-war couples move to the suburbs and start entertaining again than the cocktail hour, and the Martini, were reborn.

Health and safety concerns took their toll in the mid 1980s and a three-Martini lunch became a plague that had to be wiped out. The alcohol-laden lunch is history; the Martini isn't.

The current desire for moderation includes fitness, health, and a Martini indulgence. Indeed, America is in the midst of a Martini craze fueled by nostalgia, creativity, and a desire for intense sensations. And what could deliver a more potent experience than a frosted glass of gin with a kiss of dry vermouth?

Ultimately you'll have to decide which recipe you prefer. That's part of the fun. The Absolute Beginner recipe calls for a stirred Martini. Shaking creates little shards of ice that temporarily cloud a Martini. However, those crystals of flavor may be just what you want.

With that in mind, don't think of the following recipe as the only type of Martini you can make. It's a launch pad for creativity.

Ice cubes

2 ounces (¼ cup) gin

½ teaspoon dry vermouth

1 medium pimiento-stuffed olive

Fill a tumbler two-thirds full with ice. Add gin and vermouth. Stir to mix and chill ingredients. Strain into a chilled cocktail glass. Garnish with olive.

Serves 1.

Helpful Hint

Pickle olives in gin and add punch to your Martini. Start with a small jar of olives. Drain off the brine and refill with liquor. Cover, refrigerate and use within two weeks.

Note: You'll notice the "V" word wasn't mentioned here. Vodka Martinis are a relatively new taste preference. Vodka makes a bracing, dry drink, but without the nuance of gin. If you're a Martini virgin, start with gin. Give it a try, using the best-quality gin you can afford. Then, if you prefer, switch to vodka.

MINT JULEP

A Derby party isn't complete without a round of Mint Juleps. This potable salute to the South originated in Virginia in the 1800s. To be authentic, a Julep should be made and served in a special silver cup—all the better to retain the cold. But you can substitute a highball glass.

10 large mint leaves

1 teaspoon superfine sugar

½ teaspoon water

Crushed ice

2 ounces (¼ cup) bourbon

1 mint sprig

In a tumbler, combine mint leaves, sugar, and water. Use a muddler to finely mash the mixture together until aromatic. Transfer mixture to a chilled julep cup. Fill cup half full with crushed ice. Add bourbon, stir, and then add another layer of ice to fill to within 1 inch of top. Garnish with mint sprig. Serve with a straw.

Serves 1.

OLD-FASHIONED

This salute to blended whiskies was created in Louisville, Kentucky, the heart of bourbon country, in the late 1800s.

1 sugar cube

2 drops bitters

1 teaspoon water

Ice cubes

2 ounces (¼ cup) blended whiskey

Orange or lemon twist

Maraschino cherry

Place sugar cube in the bottom of an old-fashioned glass. Add bitters and water. Using a muddler, crush sugar and bitters together. Fill glass half full with ice. Pour on whiskey. Stir. Add orange twist and cherry.

Serves 1.

PIÑA COLADA

This strained pineapple and rum drink, which originated in Puerto Rico, should be thick and frothy. The best way to develop that "smoothie" consistency is with a combination of juice and fresh fruit. If you prefer, however, skip the fresh pineapple and double the juice.

2   ounces (¼ cup) unsweetened pineapple juice

½   cup fresh diced pineapple

3   ounces (¼ cup) light rum

2   ounces (¼ cup) coconut milk

1   tablespoon sugar

½   cup crushed ice

2   pineapple wedges

Helpful Hint

Fresh pineapple has a sweet, fruity fragrance. To prepare a pineapple for Piña Coladas, remove the crown with a sharp knife. Stand the pineapple upright and peel down with a paring knife, removing the prickly skin. Cut the pineapple in half lengthwise, then into 4 to 6 long wedges per half. Remove the hard core section. One or two wedges equal ¹/₂ cup diced pineapple. Use remaining spears for garnish.

In a blender container, combine pineapple juice, pine-apple, rum, coconut milk, and sugar. Blend for a few seconds. Add crushed ice and blend until frothy, about 10 seconds. Pour into two piña colada glasses or wine glasses. Garnish with pineapple wedges. Serve with straws.

Serves 2.

ROB ROY

This Scotch-based cousin of a Manhattan is named for the Scottish hero Robert Macgregor, also known as Rob Roy. Roy is Scottish slang for a man with red hair, so don't omit the red cherry from this drink.

Ice cubes

1½ ounces (3 table-spoons) Scotch

1½ ounces (3 table-spoons) sweet ver-mouth

2   dashes bitters

1   maraschino cherry

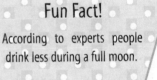

Fun Fact!

According to experts people drink less during a full moon.

Fill an old-fashioned glass half full with ice. Add Scotch, sweet vermouth, and bitters. Stir. Garnish with cherry.

Serves 1.

RUSTY NAIL

This 1950's cocktail combines the sweetness of Drambuie with the smoky taste of Scotch. Some pundits suggest the drink was named for the stirring rod—a rusty nail! More likely the name reflects the drink's rust color.

Ice cubes

1 ounce (2 tablespoons) Scotch

¼ ounce (½ tablespoon) Drambuie

Fill a shaker half full with ice cubes. Pour in Scotch and Drambuie. Shake well. Strain into a cocktail glass.

Serves 1.

SCREWDRIVER

Drink lore says this traditional brunch cocktail was created by an oilman who stirred together orange juice and liquor with a screwdriver while working in the Middle East.

Ice cubes

1½ ounces (3 tablespoons) vodka

4 ounces (½ cup) fresh orange juice

1 orange slice

Helpful Hint

You'll see blood oranges, with juice the color of rubies, in better supermarkets starting late winter. Substitute blood orange juice for the usual orange juice in the Screwdriver for stunning results. Blood oranges are tangier than Florida juice oranges, so add 1 to 2 teaspoons simple syrup to the recipe.

Fill a highball glass two-thirds full with ice. Pour in vodka, then orange juice. Stir. Garnish with orange slice.

Serves 1.

SIDECAR

Inspired by the motorbike sidecar that was so fashionable in Europe after World War I, a Parisian bartender created this piquant combination of brandy and Cointreau.

Ice cubes

1½ ounces (3 tablespoons) brandy

¾ ounce (1½ tablespoons) Cointreau

¾ ounce (1½ tablespoons) fresh lemon juice

Fill a shaker half full with ice cubes. Add brandy, Cointreau, and lemon juice. Shake well. Strain into a cocktail glass.

Serves 1.

Between the Sheets

The Sidecar may be the father to Between the Sheets, the Flapper sensation of the 1930s. Like a Sidecar, Between the Sheets is a combination of brandy, Cointreau, and lemon juice. Depending on the source, the drink also calls for a shot of rum or gin. The proportions are 1 ounce (2 tablespoons) each of brandy, Cointreau, and rum or gin, plus ½ ounce (1 tablespoon) of lemon juice.

TOM COLLINS

The original version of this summer favorite used Old Tom Gin, which is slightly sweet. Although the name remains, most bartenders use dry gin.

Ice cubes

2   ounces (¼ cup) gin

1   teaspoon superfine sugar

¾   ounce (1½ tablespoons) lemon juice

6   ounces (¾ cup) club soda, chilled

Lemon or lime wedge

Fill a collins glass two-thirds full with ice. Add gin, sugar, and lemon juice. Stir well. Top with club soda. Stir gently once or twice. Add lemon wedge.

Serves 1.

Note: If you skip the club soda, you'll have the makings of another cocktail, the Lemon Drop (see chapter 5).

WHISKEY SOUR

Sours date back to the 1800s when brandy—not whiskey—was the liquor of choice. You could substitute brandy as a delicious alternative.

Ice

½   ounce (1 tablespoon) simple syrup

2   ounces (¼ cup) whiskey

1   ounce (2 tablespoons) fresh lemon juice

1   orange slice

1   maraschino cherry

Fill a shaker half full with ice. Add simple syrup, whiskey, and lemon juice. Cover and shake well. Strain into a sour glass. Add orange slice to the rim of the glass and float a cherry in the drink.

> **Helpful Hint**
>
> To accentuate the puckering fresh taste of citrus in your drinks, rub glass rims with either a wedge of lemon or lime.

Serves 1.

PARTIES BY THE PITCHER: RECIPES FOR LARGER QUANTITIES

You'll find it very convenient to serve pitcher and punch drinks when you've got more guests than hands for pouring. Set out a pitcher of iced drinks or a punch bowl, ladle, and cups and let guests help themselves. Choose a lively combination of fruit or fruit juices, wine or spirits, and club soda. Make lighter mixes for afternoons or summer evenings; bring out the liquors for winter parties.

You can partially assemble your recipe—mixing flavorings and noncarbonated liquids—a couple of hours in advance and chill. Add sparkling wine and/or club soda just before serving.

BLACK VELVET

This mixture of rich stout with its hint of chocolate and champagne was created during the Edwardian period in England. It's traditionally served as an accompaniment to oysters.

2 bottles (12 ounces each) Guinness stout, chilled

1 bottle (750 milliliters) brut champagne, chilled

Pour stout into a tall, chilled pitcher. Pour in champagne. Serve immediately.

Serves 6 to 8.

CHAMPAGNE PUNCH

If you're going to serve only one potent drink at a party, make it this seductive mixture of citrus and brandy, using the best-quality ingredients you can find.

8 ounces (1 cup) brandy, chilled

8 ounces (1 cup) Grand Marnier, chilled

2 ounces (¼ cup) simple syrup, chilled

4 ounces (¼ cup) fresh orange juice, chilled

Block of ice

2 bottles (750 milliliters each) brut champagne, chilled

In a large punch bowl combine brandy, Grand Marnier, simple syrup, and orange juice. Stir well. Add a block of ice. Stir again. Pour in champagne.

Serves 12 to 14.

Note: If desired, float thin orange slices in the punch.

EGGNOG

Rich egg drinks, formerly elixirs for children and the infirm, are now the choice of adults wanting the comforting, familiar tastes of their youth. Because raw eggs carry a slight risk of salmonella, substitute a pasteurized liquid egg equivalent.

1   cup liquid egg (equivalent of 4 eggs)

⅓   cup sugar

½   teaspoon vanilla extract

1½ cups milk, chilled

1½ cups half-and-half, chilled

8   ounces (1 cup) brandy, chilled

Cinnamon

In a bowl, whisk together egg equivalent and sugar. Stir in vanilla extract. Pour into a chilled pitcher. Add milk, half-and-half, and brandy. Stir well. Pour into 8 chilled old-fashioned glasses. Top each serving with a dusting of cinnamon.

Serves 8.

Fun Fact!

The drink known as a Cup, which dates back at least 100 years, consists of iced wine mixed with a spirit or liqueur and topped with club soda and seasonal fruit. It's traditionally served in a glass jug.

ORANGE-CHAMPAGNE CUP

This summer cooler is traditionally served in a glass jug. So bring on the pitcher and the jelly glasses and lift your cups . . . but not too many. Perhaps the expression "down in your cups" came from the morose feeling you get from overdrinking.

1   orange, peeled, seeded, and cut into chunks

2   ounces (¼ cup) Grand Marnier

Ice cubes

16   ounces (2 cups) sparkling rose wine, chilled

8   ounces (1 cup) club soda, chilled

4   orange wedges

Combine orange pieces and Grand Marnier in a small pitcher or tumbler. Stir and set aside 5 minutes for fruit to soak up the Grand Marnier. Pour into a large pitcher half filled with ice.

Add sparkling wine and club soda. Pour into 4 chilled jelly glasses. Garnish each serving with an orange wedge.

Serves 4.

PLANTER'S PUNCH

A true Planter's Punch is a spiced up combination of rum and orange juice, no sparkling wine. But if you want to add a little impact, a sparkling wine does the trick deliciously.

4   ounces (½ cup) dark rum

8   ounces (1 cup) orange juice, chilled

2   teaspoons superfine sugar

½   teaspoon grenadine

⅛   teaspoon bitters, optional

1   teaspoon lemon juice

16   ounces (2 cups) sparkling wine, well chilled

Combine rum, orange juice, sugar, grenadine, bitters, and lemon juice in a tall pitcher. Chill for 2 hours. Just before serving, pour in sparkling wine.

Serves 6.

RUM PUNCH

For one West Indies hostess of the 1800s, the winning rum punch included 1,200 bottles of rum, 1,200 bottles of sweet Malaga wine, 400 quarts of boiling water, 600 pounds of sugar, 200 nutmegs, plus the juice of 2,600 lemons. The punch was poured into a marble basin built into her garden. The server, sitting in a mahogany boat, rowed from guest to guest pouring punch.

The Rum Punch recipe that follows is a little more modest. However, if you are ambitious enough to dig up the rose bushes for your own rum pond, don't forget to add the club soda at the last minute.

1 ounce (2 tablespoons) fresh lemon juice

1 tablespoon superfine sugar

2 ounces (¼ cup) applejack

2 ounces (¼ cup) dark rum

8 ounces (1 cup) orange juice, chilled

8 ounces (1 cup) club soda, chilled

Ice cubes

4 orange wedges

In a tumbler, combine lemon juice and sugar. Stir well. Add applejack and rum. Stir in orange juice. Refrigerate 1 to 2 hours to chill. Pour into a pitcher. Just before serving, add club soda. Pour into collins glasses filled two-thirds full with ice. Garnish with orange wedges.

Serves 4.

SANGRIA

Noted for its blood-red color and dry but fruity taste, Sangria is one of the few punches that go well with food. Add it to the buffet table with a menu of tapas or nachos.

1   bottle (750 milliliters) dry red wine, chilled

2   ounces (¼ cup) orange-flavored liqueur

1   tablespoon superfine sugar

1   orange, thinly sliced

1   lemon, thinly sliced

Ice cubes

8   ounces (1 cup) club soda, chilled

In a pitcher, combine wine, liqueur, sugar, and orange and lemon slices. Stir well. Refrigerate 1 to 3 hours. Just before serving, pour into a second pitcher half filled with ice. Add club soda. Pour into 4 tall wine glasses, portioning a few lemon and orange slices and ice cubes into each glass.

Serves 4.

Note: Some recipes suggest you discard the lemon and orange slices before serving Sangria. But why soak fruit in a heady combination of wine and liqueur if you're not going to enjoy it?

WINE PUNCH

The base of dry red wine makes this not-too-sweet punch an excellent accompaniment to roast beef dishes.

3   bottles (750 milliliters each) dry red wine, such as Cabernet Sauvignon, chilled

¼   cup sugar

Cocktails on the Beach

Picnic cocktails? Why not? Prepare and chill a pitcher drink, such as Sangria or Rum Punch. Pour into a vacuum container. Fill a second container with ice cubes. Pack your drinks, a blanket, and a menu of cold chicken and crusty bread and take a stroll over to the beach or an outdoor concert. Make sure local ordinances allow alcoholic beverages in public recreation areas.

16 ounces (2 cups) brandy, chilled

8   ounces (1 cup) Triple Sec, chilled

4   ounces (½ cup) fresh lemon juice, chilled

Block of ice

In a cup, stir together 1 cup of the red wine with the sugar until mixture dissolves. Pour into a punch bowl. Stir in remaining wine, brandy, Triple Sec, and lemon juice. Stir again to mix well. Add a block of ice.

Serves 14 to 20.

Hot Pitcher Drinks

Make a steaming drink to take the chill off a winter party.

To prepare a drink in advance and keep it warm, pour the mixture into a slow cooker and let it simmer while you go ice skating. When your group returns, let guests help themselves.

MULLED WINE

Heat is the last thing to which you'd subject a fine, expensive Bordeaux, so use a dry $5 to $8 wine in this recipe. Mulled Wine still has some, but not all, of the alcohol content of the spirits.

1   bottle (750 milliliters) dry red wine

4   ounces (½ cup) brandy

4   ounces (½ cup) orange liqueur

¼   cup sugar

2   cinnamon sticks

2   star anise

2   oranges, unpeeled, cut into thin slices

> **Fun Fact!**
>
> Home distilleries were so common in colonial America that even George Washington and Thomas Jefferson brewed their own rye whiskey.

In a large saucepan, combine red wine, brandy, orange liqueur, sugar, cinnamon sticks, star anise, and half the orange slices. Bring to a simmer. Remove from heat when hot. Discard orange slices. Pour wine into a heatproof pitcher, for self-service, or pour into 6 mugs and top each with an orange slice.

Serves 6.

IRISH COFFEE

It was the early 1950s when airline passengers—weary, cold, and irritable—gathered at Shannon Airport in Ireland to await their flights. They wanted a drink with sustenance for the long trip ahead. The creative bartender accommodated them with piping hot coffee laced with Irish whiskey and topped with cream . . . and the rest is history. The concoction spread from Ireland to almost every bar in the United States. Irish Coffee is a great winter beverage.

2   tablespoons sugar, divided

6   ounces (¾ cup) Irish whiskey

24 ounces (3 cups) freshly brewed strong, hot coffee

½   cup whipping cream

Combine 1½ tablespoons of the sugar, whiskey, and coffee in a heatproof pitcher.

In the bowl of an electric mixer, combine remaining ½ tablespoon sugar and cream. Whip to soft peaks and spoon into a small serving bowl.

Pour coffee into 4 mugs. Top each serving with a dollop of cream.

Serves 4.

GLAMOROUS GARNISHES

The right garnish is as essential to a drink as the appropriate shirt is to an outfit. A garnish does several things:

- **It defines a drink.** See an olive in a clear liquid and you automatically assume you're getting a Martini; a celery stalk in a glass of tomato juice says Bloody Mary.
- **It adds a distinctive flavor.** Drop a rich, buttery, and briny olive into a gin and vermouth drink and you've got a Martini. Make it a slightly acidic onion and you've got a Gibson.
- **It's colorful.** Sure, serious drinkers want their cocktails straight, no "garbage"—a bartender's derisive word for a

Float Fruit in an Ice Cube

Choose maraschino cherries or canned mandarin oranges that have been processed with sugar, not the water-pack variety. Sugar-packed fruit are less likely to deteriorate when frozen. Pour water into ice-cube trays to half fill each compartment. When almost solid, remove from freezer, add fruit, and press down. Return to the freezer until the fruit is firmly embedded in the ice. Then fill each compartment with enough water to cover fruit. Freeze until solid. Use within a week.

garnish that isn't functional—but most people go for eye appeal. A mouthwatering kabob of mango and pineapple chunks decorating a Piña Colada whets the appetite.

- **It's distracting.** Let's say you're tongue-tied and can't think of what to say to the good-looking hunk you've cornered. Fidget with your garnish and you'll find the words.

You know about olives, onions, and lemon wedges. Here are some exciting new looks for your cocktail glass:

- Take a paper-thin jicama slice. Make a ½-inch slash and anchor onto a Bloody Mary. Or get really fancy: use cookie cutters to create attractive shapes from the jicama.
- Remove the pimiento from a stuffed olive and substitute a strip of pickled jalapeño chile.
- Can't decide whether you want a Martini or a Gibson? Stuff olives with cocktail onions and have the best of both tastes.

- For cucumber pinwheels, run a fork down the length of a cucumber to create long grooves. Cut thin horizontal slices from the cucumber.
- Cucumber spears are delicious garnishes just waiting for a finishing touch. Lightly dust a spear with cayenne pepper and lay it across a Bloody Mary.
- Sprinkle minced fresh mint over a pineapple wedge and add it to an Aqua Fresca.
- Float a pickled Hungarian cherry pepper in a Martini.
- Add mango kabobs to a Whiskey Sour, strawberries on a stick to a Strawberry Daiquiri, or banana slices to a Banana Daiquiri.
- Add a candy cane stirrer or chocolate-covered mint sticks to a crème de menthe drink.
- Fit small straws into scallion stems, then use these straws for Bullshots or Bloody Marys.
- Use festive floral garnishes. Chive blossoms, available during April and May, make a lively topping for a Bloody Mary. Float unsprayed rose petals on a Champagne Cocktail, and scatter nasturtiums over a Screwdriver. Before planting a cocktail garden, contact your local gardening society or county extension service and get a list of edible flowers.

> **Helpful Hint**
> Keep fruit such as bananas, apples, and peaches from browning by brushing lightly with fresh lemon juice.

Going through this chapter, you did try out a few of the sensational recipes, didn't you? You're no longer tentative at the bar. You'll not only be the mixing marvel of your own parties, but the treasured guest for other hosts as well. To polish your skills, move on to the next level of drink making.

Mixology Magic

More Adventurous Cocktails

A couple of years ago, as a jaded survivor of many Margarita-laced parties, I sipped my first Cosmopolitan while at a conference attended mostly by women. The wait staff approached with a tray of pretty, pink, innocent-looking drinks. Pink ladies' drinks! *How fifties,* I thought, accepting the chilled cocktail glass with more than a little scorn. But one sip transformed everyone, myself included, into a giddy bunch of Cosmo-crazy gals. Who would have thought a little pink drink could pack so much flavor and punch?

There's a lesson here. As much as you wrap classic drinks in history and tradition, you can't overlook exciting new drinks that are being created all the time. Once you've mastered the Martini and the Manhattan, expand your horizons and try more adventurous cocktails. When you're looking for ideas, start at your favorite bar. Bartenders are making their concoctions more compelling than ever.

Like chefs, bartenders are looking at ingredients from around the world. Encouraged by globe-traveling customers, bartenders are experimenting with different flavor combinations, spirits from other countries, and new ways of serving drinks. Who would have imagined a cocktail that calls for Kalamansi Philippine citrus juice, an unusual nectar that tastes like a combination of California Meyer lemons and mandarin oranges? Who would have imagined an infusion of the herb verbena in vodka? You'll find these and more on the bar menus of trendy watering holes.

Bartenders are also looking to restaurants' food menus for inspiration. For example, you'll find that tiramisu, the go-instantly-to-the-hips Italian dessert of mascarpone cheese, coffee, and cake is also a drink. You're not going to find bits of pureed cake in your glass. Instead, you'll bliss out on a combination of cream and coffee and chocolate liqueurs that captures the essence of the rich dessert. You'll no doubt see more associations between drinks and food in your favorite bar or bistro. Bartenders are as excited about their craft as chefs are. They work with chefs to design drinks that complement food. When you start experimenting—directions for absolute beginners follow—keep food flavors in mind.

And if you come across a bar drink you love, ask the bartender how he or she makes it. Nothing will flatter a bartender as much as your interest. You may never be inclined to duplicate a bartender's recipes. Making your own ginger beer, for example, which some professionals do, is a time-consuming process. But you'll be excited and inspired by what's being concocted. For instance, you may find some wonderful drink recipes that use store-bought ginger beer.

As you've probably figured out, drinks follow fashions just like hemlines and tie widths. One mixologist offers the theory that folks like simple, straight drinks during Republican administrations and complex cocktails when a Democratic chief is at the helm. Is there any truth to this? Check it out at your next party. See if your friends' politics match their drink choices.

Right now, sweet and tart drinks such as the Cosmopolitan are in. Concoctions that use herbs, spices, infusions, and fruit liqueurs are also making the pages of bar menus. Who knows what that says about cocktail lovers. But don't be a slave to drink fashions. Shake and sip until you find the flavors you love.

RECIPES FOR THE ADVENTUROUS

BELLINI

Venice in the 1940s was impoverished by war, but that didn't stop the genius Giuseppe Cipriani, bartender of Harry's Bar, from creating his luscious and lively peach cocktail.

2   teaspoons lemon juice

2   ounces (¼ cup) peach nectar, chilled

4   ounces (½ cup) brut champagne, chilled

1   peach slice, peeled

In a flute glass, pour in lemon juice and peach nectar. Stir. Fill glass with champagne. Add peach slice for garnish.

Serves 1.

Note: Try the very sweet, very perfumed white peach varieties in a Bellini. Bella!

Helpful Hint

During the summer, when fresh peaches beckon with their perfume, stock up on the fruit and make your own peach nectar. Peel ripe peaches, then puree in a blender or food processor. Press the puree through a mesh strainer into a bowl. Discard the pulp.

CHOCOTINI

Serve this delightful concoction as an after-dinner drink. For an instant and sensational dessert, add a small dollop of premium fudge-ripple ice cream to the glass. Serve with demitasse spoons.

4 teaspoons confectioners' sugar

1 teaspoon unsweetened cocoa

Ice cubes

2 ounces (¼ cup) vodka

½ ounce (1 tablespoon) chocolate liqueur

In a fine mesh sieve, combine sugar and cocoa. Shake out onto a flat plate.

Wet the rim of a cocktail glass with water. Dip the rim into the sugar combination to coat. Set glass aside 10 minutes to dry. If time allows, chill in refrigerator 1 hour.

Fill a tumbler two-thirds full with ice. Add vodka and liqueur. Shake. Strain into prepared glass.

Serves 1.

Note: For a Chocomintini, add 1 teaspoon clear crème de menthe or 1 to 2 drops mint extract to the vodka and liqueur mixture.

> ### Fun Fact!
> The word "distill" comes from the Latin, "destillare," which means "to trickle down."

COSMOPOLITAN

This pretty and potent drink practically defined the cocktail revival of the 1990s. Use both a high-quality cranberry juice and fresh lime juice for tart accents.

Ice cubes

2   ounces (¼ cup) vodka

½   ounce (1 tablespoon) Triple Sec

1   ounce (2 tablespoons) cranberry juice

¾   ounce (1½ tablespoons) fresh lime juice

1   to 2 teaspoons superfine sugar

Fill shaker half full with ice cubes. Add vodka, Triple Sec, cranberry juice, and lime juice. Add 1 teaspoon sugar. Shake well. Taste and add remaining sugar if necessary. Shake again. Strain into oversized cocktail glass.

Serves 1.

Note: The amount of sugar you add depends on the tartness of the cranberry and lime juices. Aim for a drink that has a hint of tartness.

DINOSAUR-TINI

Use the fruit that's sometimes called a "dinosaur" plum. The plumcot, a hybrid of an apricot and plum, offers just the sweetness, juicy texture, and deep red color you'll want in this drink.

1   very large red plumcot, peeled, pitted, and diced

1   tablespoon sugar or more to taste

2   ounces (¼ cup) light rum

4   ice cubes

In a bowl, stir together plum and 1 tablespoon sugar. Set aside 30 minutes for plum to break down.

Place plum mixture in blender. Add rum and ice. Blend until pureed. Taste. If plum is very sour, add 1 teaspoon sugar and blend again. Pour into a margarita glass.

Serves 1.

FINOTINI

Many people consider fino to be the finest-quality sherry. It's pale, delicate, and dry. It is sold at various stages of aging. Don't substitute pale, cream sherry in this drink.

Ice cubes

2 ounces (¼ cup) gin

1 teaspoon fino sherry

1 lemon peel twist

In a tumbler half filled with ice, combine gin and sherry. Stir several times. Strain into a cocktail glass. Add lemon twist as garnish.

Serves 1.

> **Helpful Hint**
>
> If someone asks for a lowball, put the shaker away. A lowball is another term for a stirred drink such as a Martini or Gin Gimlet.

FROZEN RASPBERRY DAIQUIRI

Use this recipe as a basic formula for other fruit daiquiris, such as strawberry or peach. Substitute a quarter cup diced, frozen fruit, packed without sugar, if fresh fruit is unavailable.

¾ ounce (1½ tablespoons) lemon juice

½ ounce (1 tablespoon) simple syrup (see note)

2 ounces (¼ cup) light rum

¼ cup fresh raspberries

4 ice cubes

In a cup, combine lemon juice, simple syrup, and rum. Stir well to blend. Pour into a blender. Add raspberries and ice cubes. Blend until ice cubes are crushed and drink is frothy, about 30 seconds. Pour into a margarita glass.

Serves 1.

Note: If raspberries are tart, add a touch more simple syrup.

HAVANA DELIGHT

This favorite of Carnival Cruise Line clients is served on tours around the Caribbean islands. Be sure to use coconut cream, not milk, for richer results.

¾ ounce (1½ tablespoons) light rum

¾ ounce (1½ tablespoons) Kahlúa

1½ ounces (3 tablespoons) coconut cream

¾ cup ice cubes

Nasturtium for garnish

In blender, whir together rum, Kahlúa, coconut cream, and ice cubes. Mix for 30 seconds or until smooth. Pour into a margarita glass and garnish with a nasturtium.

Serves 1.

Helpful Hint

Coconut products give cocktails a sweet, nutty taste and creamy texture. Three different coconut liquids are popular in Caribbean drinks: coconut milk, which is made by processing equal parts coconut meat and water; coconut cream, which has a higher proportion of coconut; and cream of coconut, a pre-sweetened mixture of coconut and water. For rich drinks, use coconut cream; for lighter beverages, choose the milk. Reserve cream of coconut for desserts or dessert drinks.

Helpful Hint

The intense lemon essence is in the peel. You're wasting the peel if you just drop it into a drink. First rub the rim of the glass with the peel. Then twist the peel over the drink to release a few drops of lemon oil. You can go one step further and run a lit match over the lemon peel to help release the oil. Then add it to the cocktail.

KIR ROYALE

Just a tad of French black currant liqueur transforms brut champagne into a delightful drink any time of the year.

1   teaspoon crème de cassis

4   ounces (½ cup) dry or brut champagne, chilled

Pour crème de cassis into a flute glass. Pour in champagne.

Serves 1.

Note: For Kir, use dry white wine instead of champagne.

LEMON DROP

This drink has several variations, including one with Absolut Citron vodka. I prefer the bracing taste of fresh lemon juice. If you prefer less "zip," add another teaspoon of superfine sugar.

1   tablespoon granulated sugar

Ice cubes

2   ounces (¼ cup) gin or vodka

2   teaspoons superfine sugar

¾   ounce (1½ tablespoons) lemon juice

Lemon wedge

Spread granulated sugar on a small plate. Wet the rim of a cocktail glass and dip it into the sugar to coat. Turn glass upright and allow to dry. If possible, chill glass in refrigerator. Fill a shaker two-thirds full with ice. Add gin, sugar, and lemon juice. Shake vigorously and strain into prepared glass. Garnish with lemon wedge.

Serves 1.

MIMOSA

This combination of champagne, orange liqueur, and orange juice was named for the apricot-colored mimosa flower. Although the cocktail dates back to the 1920s, its flavor is fresh and contemporary.

Ice cubes

1   ounce (2 tablespoons) Grand Marnier

2   ounces (¼ cup) fresh-squeezed orange juice, well chilled

4   ounces (½ cup) brut champagne, well chilled

Fill a shaker half full with ice cubes. Add Grand Marnier and orange juice. Shake well. Strain into an old-fashioned glass. Pour in champagne. Stir gently 2 to 3 times.

Serves 1.

NEGRONI CHAMPAGNE COCKTAIL

Campari, an Italian bitter, didn't catch on in the United States until it was tamed by the pleasing taste of sweet vermouth. The classic Negroni doesn't use champagne, but see if a bit of the bubbly doesn't make this drink livelier.

Ice cubes

1½ ounces (3 tablespoons) gin

1½ ounces (3 tablespoons) sweet vermouth

1½ ounces (3 tablespoons) Campari

6 ounces (¾ cup) brut champagne, chilled

2 orange wedges

Fill a shaker half full with ice cubes. Add the gin, vermouth, and Campari. Shake well and strain into two cocktail glasses. Fill each with half the champagne. Top each glass with an orange wedge.

Serves 2.

RUMTINI

Despite its long history—rum-making dates back to the seventeenth century—rum is suddenly trendy. Bartenders like rum because it's so versatile. You'll like it because it's so smooth, as you'll see in this stunning blue cocktail.

Ice cubes

2   ounces (¼ cup) light rum

½   ounce (1 tablespoon) blue curaçao

1   teaspoon Grand Marnier

Fill a tumbler half full with ice. Add rum, curaçao, and Grand Marnier. Stir a few times. Strain into a cocktail glass.

Serves 1.

SAKETINI

Interest in Pan-Asian and fusion cooking inspired this combination of sake and vodka that has a rounder, less sharp taste than the usual martini.

Ice cubes

2   ounces (¼ cup) vodka

½   ounce (1 tablespoon) sake

1   lemon twist

Fill a tumbler two-thirds full with ice. Add vodka and sake. Stir several times. Strain into a cocktail glass. Add lemon twist.

Serves 1.

SOUR APPLE MARTINI

You'll find many versions for a Sour Apple Martini. Some taste like an alcoholic candy apple, others like a Jolly Rancher hard candy. If you want a drink on the sweet side, choose applejack. If you want a puckery cocktail, opt for sour apple schnapps. The drink that follows is a compromise between the two extremes.

Ice cubes

1 ounce (2 tablespoons) vodka

1 ounce (2 tablespoons) applejack

1 tablespoon superfine sugar

1 teaspoon fresh lemon juice

1 green apple wedge

Fill a shaker half full with ice. Add vodka, applejack, sugar, and lemon juice. Shake well and strain into a cocktail glass. Garnish with apple wedge.

Serves 1.

Fun Fact!

Put an old-fashioned flip on the list of drinks banned by the "food cops." A flip made by proper hostesses in the 1700s started with 32 egg yolks, whisked with an equal number of spoonfuls of sugar. The fluffy mass was diluted with brandy, Madeira, sherry, and five pints of cream. Is it any wonder people didn't live to a ripe old age back then?

SPRING TULIP

Inspired by the Cosmo craze, this cocktail gets a bubbly champagne finish. If you can't find cranberry liqueur, substitute apricot brandy.

Ice cubes

2 ounces (¼ cup) vodka, chilled

1 teaspoon cranberry liqueur

½ ounce (1 tablespoon) sweet-and-sour mix

2 ounces (¼ cup) champagne, chilled

Fill a tumbler two-thirds full with ice. Add vodka, cranberry liqueur, and sweet-and-sour mix. Stir several times. Strain into a flute glass. Add champagne.

Serves 1.

VODKA SOUR

An old favorite, the salty dog, a combination of gin or vodka and grapefruit juice, inspired this breathtaking, zesty cocktail that's a play on trendy herb-seasoned drinks. Adjust the sugar according to your taste.

1   tablespoon finely chopped mint leaves

1   lime wedge

Ice cubes

2   teaspoons superfine sugar

2   ounces (¼ cup) vodka, chilled

1   ounce (2 tablespoons) fresh grapefruit juice

1   lime slice for garnish

In a shaker, combine mint leaves and lime wedge. Use a muddler to mash the mint with the lime. Fill shaker half full with ice. Add sugar, vodka, and grapefruit juice. Cover shaker and shake well. Strain into a cocktail glass and garnish with lime slice.

Serves 1.

WHISKEY SMASH

If you love the tangy kick of a Whiskey Sour, try this variation using a fresh lemon. Muddling releases the lemon's essential oils and permeates the whiskey with an intense citrus fragrance.

½   lemon

1   tablespoon superfine sugar

1   ounce (2 tablespoons) fresh orange juice

Ice cubes

2   ounces (¼ cup) Irish whiskey

1   orange slice

In a tumbler, combine lemon, sugar, and orange juice. Muddle together. Fill an old-fashioned glass two-thirds full with ice. Add the lemon mixture with the crushed lemon. Add whiskey and stir well. Garnish glass with orange slice.

Serves 1.

Fun Fact!

In Fairbanks, Alaska, it's illegal to give a moose an alcoholic drink.

Pousse-Café: The Layered Look

Pousse-Café (rhymes with loose café) is a drink in which one liquid is layered on top of another. Your guests will think this is a miraculous feat. How can one liquid float on top of another? The secret is in the specific weight or density of each liquid. To create a layered drink, start by adding the heaviest liquid, then a lighter one, and so on, until you have as many layers as the drink will hold before all the liquids flow together.

Depending on your skill and patience, you can create two, three, or even four layers. The results are dazzling and luscious. Your guests will sip one layer at a time, marveling at how each drink was constructed.

A Pousse-Café takes patience and a steady hand. This is a drink you'll make one at a time for a small group.

A Pousse-Café is made in a special, straight-sided glass of the same name. The glass design helps the layers maintain their shape. Most drinks call for liqueurs, which tend to have a higher density than liquors. Unfortunately labels don't give density ratings for liqueurs. You'll learn this by following the directions below and through trial and error.

Don't try this in public until you've had some practice. Choose a quiet work space with no vibrations. Set up your materials before you begin. Make sure your glassware is thoroughly clean and dried.

Start with a pousse-café glass or substitute a champagne flute. Pour in ½ ounce (1 tablespoon) of the densest liqueur you'll use. The layer should be ¼- to ½-inch deep.

Next place a long-handled, narrow spoon into the glass, just touching the liquid. As you add your next layer, another ½-ounce portion, trickle it over the back of the spoon. This prevents the second layer from breaking into the first. Wipe the spoon handle clean and add a third layer if you dare. You may want to use a twisted-handle bar spoon, which slows the flow of the liquid into the glass.

As you compose a Pousse-Café, think of the flavors and colors. Choose liqueurs in deep ruby red, forest green, lemon yellow. Use the following as a guide to your flavor and color scheme. The liquids are ranked by weight, starting with the heaviest and ending with the lightest:

Anisette (clear)
Grenadine (ruby red)
Crème de menthe (green or clear)
Crème de cacao (brown or clear)
Coffee liqueur (brown)
Cherry liqueur (red)

Blue curaçao (blue)
Blackberry liqueur (very deep purple)
Grand Marnier (golden)
Sloe gin (red)
Kirsch (clear)
Brandy (golden)

Vary the flavors or stick with a theme. For example, use only fruit, such as cherry and orange, or concentrate on fun, sweet liqueurs, such as crème de cacao and crème de menthe.

If your drink layers break as you're pouring, stop, take a sip to make sure you like the concoction, then pour out the mixture and start again.

As a general rule, if you'd like to use a flavoring syrup, such as grenadine, start with it; syrups are heavier than liqueurs. Next add the liqueur, then the liquor, such as brandy or scotch. If you'd like a rich ending to the drink, add a layer of cream. It floats to the top.

Here are a couple of delicious combinations:

CHERRY-ORANGE DELIGHT

½ ounce (1 tablespoon) Peter Heering

½ ounce (1 tablespoon) Grand Marnier

½ ounce cream

Layer in order, following suggestions, into a poussecafé glass.

Serves 1.

CHOCOLATE-CREAM CHERRY

½ ounce (1 tablespoon) Peter Heering

½ ounce (1 table- spoon) light crème de cacao

1 tablespoon cream

Layer in order, following suggestions, into a poussecafé glass.

Serves 1.

Fun Fact!

Pousse-Café means "pushes coffee" in French, making it an ideal after-dinner drink.

RING AROUND THE GLASS RIM

You know how appealing the sensation of salt and sweet can be in a cocktail. Your mouth moves from the salt-glazed rim of a margarita glass to the sweet Triple Sec and tequila combination to come. Salt is just the start to glazes you can use to flavor and decorate glass rims.

There are many wonderful, colorful options. Don't limit yourself to margarita glasses. You can use this for sparkling wine drinks, Martinis, and Daiquiris as well as Margaritas. To start, wet the rim of a glass. Spoon a flavoring ingredient onto a saucer. Dip the glass rim in the flavoring, turn the glass right-side up and let it dry.

Here are some starters:

> To celebrate holidays or birthdays, use colored sugar to rim glasses for a Daiquiri, Whiskey Sour, or one of the Pousse-Café drinks. Use red and green sugars for Christmas, pink for a gal-pal party, and blue for the boys.
>
> Place 2 tablespoons sweetened cocoa on a plate. Dip a glass for a chocolate-based Pousse-Café such as an Angel's Tip (which is equal parts dark crème de cacao and half-and-half).
>
> Use 2 tablespoons sweetened cocoa for a Chocotini.
>
> For a White Russian, which is vodka, coffee liqueur, and cream, stir together a combination of one part powdered hot chocolate mix, a dash of powdered instant espresso, and a dash of cinnamon.
>
> For a Mintini—vodka with a hint of crème de menthe— use finely minced fresh mint.
>
> And how about a Hotini? Put crushed red pepper flakes on a dish and coat your glass. Pour in *The Absolute Beginner's* Martini, but be sure to warn your guests they're getting a scorcher.

MAKING YOUR OWN MIXERS

You can buy or make simple syrup to sweeten your drinks or sweet-and-sour mix for the one-two punch of a Whiskey Sour, but you should know how to make your own. You'll have fresher, better-tasting products that cost less. And you'll know what to do if you run out of mix as the crowd is lined up for cocktails.

> ### Helpful Hint
> When your mouth is blazing from the aftereffects of chiles, eat a slice of bread to extinguish the flames. Drinking water only sends the volatile oils coursing through your system.

SWEET-AND-SOUR MIX

1½ ounces (3 table-
   spoons) simple syrup

4   ounces (½ cup) fresh lemon juice

4   ounces (½ cup) fresh lime juice

1½ ounces (3 tablespoons) water

Combine ingredients in a measuring cup. Stir well. Pour into a glass container, cover tightly with lid and refrigerate up to one month.

Makes 1⅔ cups.

Note: If you're using sweet-and-sour mix for Daiquiris, add the grated zest of the lemon and lime to the recipe. You'll get a stronger citrus accent.

Some recipes for sweet-and-sour mix call for a raw egg white. That could increase your risk for developing a food-borne illness.

MULLING SPICES

You've got the wine on simmer and you're about to make a bone-warming pot of mulled wine, but you're out of cinnamon, or you can't find the cloves. Avoid the hassle by making a mixture of mulling spices to keep on hand.

Favorite mixtures include cinnamon sticks, cloves, allspice berries, and star anise.

12 small cinnamon sticks

4   teaspoons cloves, allspice, or star anise (or a mixture of these)

Add cinnamon sticks to a small clean jar. Mix in the 4 teaspoons of the smaller spice(s). Use 3 cinnamon sticks and a teaspoon of other spices for one pot of mulled wine or cider.

Store the spices in a cool, dry area, such as your liquor cabinet. Exchange for new spices every year.

YOUR LIQUOR LAB

Okay, maybe chemistry wasn't your favorite subject in school. That's because you weren't interested in the outcome. Releasing sulfur dioxide? Phew. But now you can conduct yummy experiments that will turn you into a master mixologist. Forget the Bunsen burner and flasks. Assemble a few of your favorite liquors and get to work.

Flavoring Spirits

Orange vodka, lime gin, and cranberry tequila. These new liquors turn your cocktails into a fruity festival for your taste buds. Imagine a Margarita with a hint of cranberry or a Vodka and Tonic with a taste of orange. Yummy. No wonder flavored spirits are filling the shelves of liquor stores. You're probably tempted to add one or two flavored spirits to your collection.

You can also make your own flavor-infused alcohol. There are several advantages to the do-it-yourself approach.

- You can make as little or as much as you'd like. You won't have to invest in a liter bottle of liquor when all you need is four ounces.
- Your infused alcohol will be custom blended with the degree of flavorings you and not a manufacturer chooses.
- You can dream up and create infusions that will never be available in your liquor store. How about lemongrass vodka for your Vodka and Tonic or cinnamon and star anise rum to use in punches? Luscious.
- You're using fresh, quality ingredients. Not to knock a commercial product, but their raspberry essence is as likely to come from a test tube as a farm.
- You don't need to spend a lot of money for costly spirits. An economical gin, vodka, tequila, or rum will be suitable. You should choose clear, mild-tasting spirits for infusion. Their neutral tastes won't fight with the seasonings you'll add. Whiskey and scotch would be wasted as infused liquors.

A few notes of caution first. Although it's very unlikely that alcohol will spoil, the ingredients and equipment you use to infuse your spirits may become contaminated with bacteria. Take some steps to prevent spoilage:

Use clean equipment. Run your heat-resistant bottles through the dishwasher at the hottest setting or set bottles on a rack in a large pot, cover with water, bring to a boil, and simmer five minutes.

Wash any ingredient you're going to use for a flavor infusion. This includes vanilla bean pods and coffee beans as well as raspberries. Rinse well under running water and let air dry.

Strain out solids from your infused spirits after a few days. Some recipes call for adding a food, such as berries, as a decoration. You're at less risk for food spoilage if you don't add anything solid to your infused spirit. Label your product with the preparation date so you know when it's time to finish it up.

Basic Recipe for Infused Spirits

To make an infused spirit, start with a 250-milliliter or 500-milliliter bottle of vodka, gin, tequila, or light rum. Pour the liquor into a clean 500-milliliter to 1-liter glass canning jar with a clean lid. Don't use an ordinary jar that can't withstand sterilizing heat or that can't be tightly closed. Add the infusion ingredient (see suggestions below). Close and shake well. Set the liquor aside in a cool, dark place for two days, shaking twice a day.

After two days, take a taste. You should notice a subtle flavor change. For a more intense flavor, soak your infusion one to three more days. Then strain out the solids and pour the flavored liquor into a clean decanter or decorator bottle. Cover with a cap and refrigerate. Infused liquors won't keep indefinitely. Use within a few months. If your product looks cloudy, discard it.

Use the following additions to one pint of liquor of choice.

- For a lemon infusion, peel off the outer colored skin of one well-washed lemon. Scrape off as much of the bitter white pith as possible before adding the lemon peel to the liquor.
- For a tangerine infusion, peel off the outer colored skin of one well-washed tangerine.
- For a coffee infusion, add 2 tablespoons coffee beans to vodka.
- For a vanilla infusion, add 2 well-washed vanilla beans to vodka or rum. For more vanilla flavor, split the beans in half lengthwise. Discard after infusing.

- For sour-apple vodka, peel off and add the skin from a large, well-washed Granny Smith apple.

EXPERIMENTING WITH COLOR

Look at the rich copper tones of finely aged bourbon. The color doesn't come from the grains used to make the spirit; nor does it come from a dye bottle. The distinctive and inviting hue comes from aging bourbon in wood barrels. Sugars and tannins in the woods leach into the liquor, tinting it.

Vodka and gin are clear because they aren't aged in wood. But what about that funky blue curaçao or that emerald green crème de menthe? Admittedly, these shades weren't influenced by nature. They came from food dyes, colorings that are approved as safe by the U.S. Food and Drug Administration.

> **Fun Fact!**
>
> Every housewife worth her ration of sugar in colonial America made "weed wines" such as dandelion, elder-blossom, and blackberry.

If you'd like to have a little fun with your spirits, add a drop or two of liquid food coloring to a bottle of clear liquor. For example, turn vodka pink or gin orange, or tint your homemade infused liquors the color of the infusion. Add, for example, a drop of orange to a bottle of vodka you flavored with orange peel.

DRINKMEISTER: INVENTING YOUR OWN COCKTAILS

Okay, you've mastered the Martini and your Margarita sets off mariachi bands; now you want to take the next step. You want to invent your own cocktails. Why you could become the next Victor Bergeron, who brought the Mai Tai to life, or Patrick Duffy, who made the highball a popular drink category.

Fun Fact!

Dish manufacturers in old England baked a whistle into the rim or handle of ceramic cups that were used in taverns. When customers wanted a refill, they tooted their whistles. Soon barhoppers referred to drinking as "wetting their whistles."

Start slowly. There's a method to mixology. Work with single-spirit drinks first. Combine a jigger of vodka, gin, rum, or tequila with a mixer and taste your experiment. Not bad? Start tinkering. Does the drink need a jolt of acid from citrus or cranberry juice, the sweetness of sugar, or the mellowing power of another spirit? Don't play with more than two or three recipes at a time. You'll find your palate gets dulled and your head throbs after a while. Write the formula of a drink recipe you really like and try it out on your friends. A cocktail is born.

SPECIAL TOUCHES

Once you've mastered the basics, try some tricks to impress your guests.

Light My Fire: Flaming Drinks

Playing with fire adds drama to dinner parties. You'll have fun and keep the setting safe if you pay close attention to what you're doing. Don't flambé liquor while you're distracted or have had too much to drink. You'll need a steady hand and clear mind.

Here are some tips before starting:

- Don't wear clothing with loose-fitting or flowing sleeves that could catch fire.
- Make sure you don't have loose gauzy fabrics or papers nearby.
- Choose heat-resistant glassware.

- Set the scene. Wait until there's a lull in the after-dinner conversation. Gather all your props, dim the lights, and perform your magic.

To flame a drink, pour 2 to 3 tablespoons high-proof liquor such as brandy, whiskey, or rum into a metal ladle. Warm gently over a candle. Do not allow to boil. Ignite the liquor with a long-stemmed match. While the liquor is flaming, pour it into a heatproof glass or into a drink, such as hot coffee or hot mulled cider, in a mug.

Wait for the flames to die, then serve. (Hey, hot lips: Never sip a blazing drink.)

Flambé each drink individually so you don't have a large, uncontrollable flame. Never pour alcohol straight from the bottle into a flaming drink. The stream of alcohol could set on fire, leading back to your hand.

Chilling Out: Frozen Drinks

During extremely hot weather you may be tempted to climb into the freezer and keep your ice cubes company. Ah, the agony. Even your standby Gin and Tonic doesn't provide much relief. But you'll chill in no time with a frozen Margarita, Daiquiri, or Gin Gimlet.

For a refreshing sherbet-like consistency, pour the liquor, then the mixers, for one drink into a blender with a strong motor (see chapter 3 for shopping tips). Add 1 cup crushed ice and turn on the motor to blend. Blend only until the mixture looks light and finely processed. If the liquid starts to separate out from the ice, add a little more crushed ice and blend briefly. Immediately pour the mixture into a chilled glass. You can double or triple the recipe, adding 1 cup of crushed ice for each drink.

Years from now you may reminisce about sipping Cosmopolitans along with the angst-driven women on the cable TV hit, *Sex and the City*. Perhaps you imbibed Harvey

What's That Scent You're Wearing?

Body cocktails are the latest craze in trendy spas, as zany as it seems. Expect to pay almost $100 to have your body exfoliated with a Martini- or Cosmopolitan-scented salt scrub. Imagine telling your loved one: "No, honey. I didn't spend the afternoon in a bar. I know I smell like a Manhattan. The liquor is the scent my masseuse uses."

If you want to experience this fad, make your own rub to share. Pick up an unscented salt or sugar exfoliant scrub cream at your local beauty supply or department store. Then create a liquor concentrate to "perfume" your scrub. Pour ½ cup whiskey or a fruit liqueur into a small saucepan. Cook over very low heat until liquor is reduced to 1 tablespoon and is syrupy. Stir into your usual scrub cream.

Wallbangers a couple of decades before, when the orange juice, vodka, and Galliano cocktail meant you were hip. Even though some drinks have notoriety, they're no less delicious or fun to serve. To the contrary, savor the "drink of the moment" and renew your taste buds.

6

No Shirley Temples

Sophisticated Nonalcoholic
and Low-Alcohol Drinks

Pity the partygoer who doesn't drink alcoholic beverages. While other guests are sipping Margaritas, Saketinis, or Manhattans, the guest who abstains is offered a Shirley Temple! The ginger ale and grenadine drink, named for the child actress of the 1930s, says "too young to drink."

No right-thinking adult is going to accept that without wincing.

Let's face it, many nonalcoholic drinks are either syrupy sweet or are stripped down, liquor-free versions of the classics, providing sometimes dubious results.

Sugary soft-drink concoctions aren't thirst quenching. The insipid flavor often clashes with party food. Offering your guests standard drinks minus their spirits can be risky. You can take the vodka out of a Bloody Mary and you've still got a zippy tomato juice drink. But take the gin and vermouth out of a Martini and all you're left with is an olive in a cocktail glass. Not very satisfying.

Of course you want to show your nondrinking guests the same ingenuity you do for those who drink, and the following recipes offer plenty of inspiration. The drinks have full-bodied flavor, engaging pastel colors, and festive bubbles without the alcohol. You'll also get tips on stocking your bar with plenty of nonalcoholic mixers.

STOCKING THE NONALCOHOLIC BAR

When you shop, include tropical fruit juices, such as guava, mango, or papaya on your grocery list. You'll marvel at how these exotic beverages blend with club soda for refreshing drinks. Your grocery store supplies a wonderful array of sparkling fruit drinks, ranging from apple to tangerine juices, to use as drink bases. And don't forget fresh fruit garnishes. Please your guests with beautiful kabob sticks of mango, melons, and peaches. Create a drink that has eye appeal and you've made the leap from a boring to an exciting nonalcoholic drink.

Your supermarket will provide inspiration for nonalcoholic drinks, but here's a shopping list to get you started:

Apple cider, both still and sparkling
Club soda
Coffee
Cream or half-and-half
Cream of coconut and
   coconut milk
Ginger ale
Grenadine
Lemons
Limes
Mango nectar
Oranges
Orange juice (Fresh-squeezed
   is best. The runner-up is
   not-from-concentrate
   orange juice.)
Papaya nectar

Helpful Hint

To peel a peach for a kabob or a drink recipe, dip it into boiling water for 30 seconds. Remove and hold under cold, running water an equal amount of time. The skin will slip off. Do this just before using the fruit or brush the flesh with lemon juice so it doesn't brown.

Passion-fruit nectar
Pineapple juice and fresh pineapple
Spices, such as cinnamon, allspice, and star anise
Tea
Tonic water

DAZZLING NONALCOHOLIC DRINK RECIPES

Most of the smashing recipes you'll read about and enjoy here don't have a history. Nonalcoholic drinks are truly contemporary, fresh, and ever-evolving according to preferences. This author hopes you'll be moved to use these as blueprints for your own collection of signature drinks.

AGUA FRESCA

The Spanish name that translates to "fresh water" in English can't describe how refreshing this drink is. Make it just before serving so it's frothy and fruity.

8 ounces (1 cup) cold water

2 cups crushed ice

2 cups diced, fresh, ripe pineapple*

4 to 5 tablespoons sugar

Juice of 1 lime

4 mint sprigs

Combine water, ice, pineapple, 4 tablespoons sugar, and lime juice in a blender and puree until smooth. Taste and add remaining tablespoon sugar if necessary. Immediately pour into wine glasses and top each with a mint sprig.

Serves 4.

* 2 cups diced pineapple is about half a medium-size pineapple. You can double the recipe but puree half at a time.

Note: Vary the fruit according to the season and make Agua Fresca all year round. Strawberries, raspberries, or peeled peaches are especially good.

APPLE KIR

Kir, the delicate pink combination of black currant liqueur and white wine, tastes just as fruity and refreshing using black currant syrup and sparkling apple cider. As a variation, substitute sparkling pear cider.

1   teaspoon black currant syrup or ½ teaspoon grenadine

2   drops bitters

6   ounces (¾ cup) sparkling apple cider, chilled

1   long cinnamon stick

Pour black currant syrup into a champagne flute. Add bitters. Add sparkling apple cider. Stir once or twice with cinnamon stick.

Serves 1.

APPLE SPARKLER

If you don't stir the cherry juice into the cider, you'll have an elegant layered drink.

1   teaspoon green or blue colored sugar (optional)

1   teaspoon cherry juice concentrate

6   ounces (¾ cup) sparkling apple cider, chilled

2   mandarin orange segments and 1 lime segment arranged on wooden skewer, for garnish

Sprinkle colored sugar on a piece of wax paper. Wet the rim of a wine glass with water. Dip the rim in sugar and set aside 5 to 10 minutes to set.

Pour cherry juice concentrate into the wine glass. Gently pour in apple cider. Stir one or two times. Garnish with citrus skewer.

Serves 1.

Helpful Hint

Keep a chilled bottle of sparkling apple cider to use for celebrations. It's as festive a beverage as champagne.

APRICOT PASSION

Passion-fruit nectar has a delicate, floral taste that is enhanced when blended with other tropical or mild-tasting juices.

2   ounces (¼ cup) apricot nectar

2   ounces (¼ cup) passion-fruit nectar

2   ounces (¼ cup) pineapple juice

1   teaspoon lime juice

1   teaspoon sugar

4   ice cubes

1   pineapple spear or lime wedge

In a blender, combine apricot and passion-fruit nectars and pineapple juice. Add lime juice and sugar. Puree 30 seconds to blend. Add ice and blend 1 minute, or until frothy. Pour into highball glass. Add pineapple spear or lime wedge.

Serves 1.

CARIBBEAN BREEZE

Smoothies, the best thing to happen to breakfast since in-stant oatmeal, can be adapted to cocktails as well. This luscious concoction has a frothy texture and a potent, fruity flavor.

1   medium banana

2   teaspoons superfine sugar

¼   teaspoon vanilla extract

2   ounces (¼ cup) coconut milk, chilled

4   ounces (½ cup) unsweetened pineapple juice, chilled

4   ice cubes

Peel and slice banana into a blender. Add sugar, vanilla extract, coconut milk, and pineapple juice. Blend 30 seconds. Add ice cubes and blend 1 minute or until light and frothy. Pour into a highball glass.

Serves 1.

GINGER SPARKLING LEMONADE

As zesty as a Jamaican ginger ale, this piquant lemonade is flavored for adult tastes. Serve it with a Caribbean menu of meat patties, jerked chicken, and plantain fritters.

1   tablespoon grated gingerroot

⅓   cup superfine sugar

1   ounce (2 tablespoons) water

4   ounces (½ cup) fresh lemon juice

16   ounces (2 cups) club soda, chilled

Ice cubes

4   lemon wheels

In small pot, combine gingerroot, 2 tablespoons sugar, and water. Bring to a simmer. Simmer 2 minutes, or until sugar is dissolved. Stir in lemon juice and remaining sugar. Turn off heat. Stir well. Chill at least 1 hour.

Spoon mixture into a small pitcher. Add club soda. Pour into collins glasses filled two-thirds full with ice. Garnish with lemon wheels.

Serves 4.

KISS OF MINT

It's the fresh mint that makes this a breathtaking drink. If you want a sharper accent to this fruity and fabulous drink, add a drop of bitters.

1   tablespoon fresh mint leaves

1   tablespoon sugar

1   cup sliced fresh, ripe strawberries

8   ounces (1 cup) orange-tangerine juice, chilled

1   drop bitters, optional

4   ice cubes

Mint sprig, for garnish

Place mint in a blender. Add sugar, strawberries, orange-tangerine juice, and bitters if desired. Blend 30 seconds. Add ice cubes and blend 1 minute, or until light and frothy. Pour into a highball glass. Garnish with mint sprig.

Serves 1.

MULLED CIDER

Apple cider and the outdoors are a natural combination. Make a vacuum container of hot cider to take to football tailgate parties or on winter hikes.

2   liters (about ½ gallon) apple cider

3   (3-inch) cinnamon sticks

1   teaspoon cloves

1   orange, washed and thinly sliced into rounds

Juice of 1 lemon

8   (6-inch) cinnamon sticks (optional)

In a large saucepan, combine apple cider, 3 cinnamon sticks, cloves, orange slices, and lemon juice. Bring to a simmer and let simmer 10 minutes.

Strain to discard solids and pour mulled cider into 8 heatproof mugs. Garnish each with a cinnamon stick.

Serves 8.

RASPBERRY CHIFFON

This has all the froth of a sherbet fruit punch but without the syrupy sweetness. For a low-calorie version, use a diet ginger ale.

1   packed cup (6-ounce container) fresh raspberries

2   tablespoons sugar

½   ounce (1 tablespoon) fresh lemon juice

20   ounces (2½ cups) ginger ale

4   to 6 ice cubes

Combine raspberries, sugar, lemon juice, and ½ cup of the ginger ale in blender. Puree 30 seconds, just to mince raspberries. Add ice cubes and puree 1 minute or until frothy. Remove and pour into pitcher or glasses. Add remaining ginger ale, stirring gently once or twice.

Serves 4.

TROPICAL SPICED TEA

Think of tea as a canvas for other flavors. Contrast tea's tannic notes with spices, honey, and tropical fruits. It's so delicious you'll never again be tempted to serve plain tea with lemon for a cocktail party.

> ## Helpful Hint
>
> If you start with frozen fruit, blender drinks will be cold, yet less diluted. To have fresh, frozen fruit on hand, cut up odds and ends of bananas, peaches, nectarines, and strawberries. Toss with lemon juice, using 1 teaspoon juice per cup of fruit. Pack into plastic bags and freeze. Add frozen fruit directly to blender.

16 ounces (2 cups) water

4   tea bags (regular black tea)

4   star anise

1   (3-inch) cinnamon stick

1½ ounces (3 tablespoons) honey

1   ounce (2 tablespoons) lemon juice

8   ounces (1 cup) mango nectar

In a medium pot, bring water to a boil. Add tea bags, star anise, and cinnamon stick. Reduce heat to low and simmer 3 to 5 minutes. Discard tea bags and cinnamon stick. Remove star anise from pot but set aside. Stir in honey, lemon juice, and mango nectar. Simmer 5 minutes, or until hot.

Pour tea into 4 heatproof cups, topping each with a star anise.

Serves 4.

FULL-FLAVORED, LOW-ALCOHOL DRINKS

Frequently, occasions call for drinks that have just a touch of alcohol. For example, guests may prefer lighter drinks at brunches or afternoon summer parties when the combination of heat and potent alcoholic drinks can be dizzying. You'll also discover that some people feel the effects of alcohol more quickly and prefer lower-alcohol concoctions. The following recipes have all the style of mainstream cocktails, but with less alcohol.

GINGER CHAMPAGNE

Choose a ginger ale that's so dry you won't be able to whistle after a sip. Some Jamaican varieties are excellent, delivering spice, not sugar.

2 ounces (¼ cup) dry ginger ale, chilled

2 ounces (¼ cup) brut champagne, chilled

1 teaspoon chopped candied ginger (optional)

Pour ginger ale into a champagne flute. Add champagne. Stir one or two times. Drop in candied ginger.

Serves 1.

MOJITO

Along with Americans' passion for Latin-American food, is a thirst for Mojito *(MO-he-toh), a Cuban rum drink with a breathtaking hint of mint. Get out your muddler.*

2 teaspoons sugar

¼ cup mint leaves

6 ounces (¾ cup) club soda, chilled

Ice cubes

2 ounces (¼ cup) light rum

1 small lime, preferably a key lime, halved

1 mint sprig

Place sugar, mint leaves, and 1 ounce (2 tablespoons) of the club soda in a tumbler. Muddle mixture until mint leaves are crushed and very fragrant. If you can't smell the mint, keep muddling.

Spoon the mixture into a highball glass filled two-thirds full with ice. Pour in rum. Squeeze juice of lime into drink. Drop half of the lime into drink, discarding the remaining half. Fill glass with remaining club soda. Stir once or twice. Garnish with mint sprig.

Serves 1.

Fun Fact!

A mist is a drink served over shaved ice in a rocks glass. Crème de cassis mist would be a shot of the liqueur over shaved ice. Yummm. This author is sure you'll like it better than sugary snowcones.

VERMOUTH AND SODA

Vermouth, originally a medicinal spirit, is a welcome aperitif before meals. It's also a pleasurable afternoon drink.

Ice cubes

1 ounce (2 tablespoons) dry vermouth

4 ounces (½ cup) club soda

1 lemon wedge

Fill an old-fashioned glass half full with ice. Pour in vermouth. Add club soda. Stir one or two times. Garnish glass with lemon wedge.

Serves 1.

WATERMELON COOLER

Pureed watermelon is frothy, light, and thirst quenching when mixed into a white wine cocktail. If you want to make this drink really easy, purchase diced watermelon from your supermarket's salad bar.

1   cup seeded, cubed watermelon, chilled
4   ice cubes
4   ounces (½ cup) fruity white wine, chilled
4   ounces (½ cup) bitter lemon carbonated mixer (such as Schweppes), chilled

In a blender, combine watermelon with ice cubes. Blend until frothy. Pour in white wine. Pour into margarita glasses. Fill each with half the bitter lemon mixer. Stir once or twice.

Serves 2.

WHITE WINE SPRITZER

Germans introduced the world to this refreshing, sprightly summer drink. Try a chenin blanc or sauvignon blanc as the wine base.

Ice cubes
4   ounces (½ cup) fruity white wine, chilled
4   ounces (½ cup) club soda, chilled

1   teaspoon fresh lime juice

1   lime wedge

Fill a collins glass two-thirds full with ice. Pour in white wine. Add club soda and lime juice. Stir one or two times. Add lime wedge as garnish.

Serves 1.

You don't have to host a party to serve low-alcohol and nonalcoholic drinks. Treat yourself to the pleasures of fruit juices or wine enlivened with a touch of club soda as a before-dinner drink. The more often you make these drinks, the more you'll appreciate recipes that deliver light, refreshing tastes.

To Your Health

Tips for Responsible Drinking

Can you imagine an elixir that cures impotence and mental disorders while stimulating your appetite? The medical wizards of the Middle Ages believed alcohol did all that and more. Modern scientists have a more conservative perspective, but even they feel an occasional drink can be health-promoting.

There's a physical benefit to alcohol. A drink a day once you hit age fifty may keep your arteries from aging, according to Michael F. Roizen, M.D., an expert on the aging process, in his book *RealAge* (Cliff Street Books).

The psychological aspect of drinking may be just as beneficial. When you share laughter, camaraderie, and an occasional drink with your friends, you're happier. Your stress levels decline. According to Dr. Roizen, seeing friends more than once a month can actually make you feel younger. And if you get together over a glass of wine you may be enjoying its protective qualities as well.

Unfortunately, not everyone responds positively to alcohol. Some people are physiologically or psychologically less able to handle it. For some, alcohol is an addicting drug that must be avoided. Alcohol can negatively affect moods, making people morose and depressed after a drink or two, or so uninhibited, they're destructive.

People on medications can set themselves up for fatal reactions if they consume alcohol. Women who are or are trying to become pregnant shouldn't trade their babies' health for a drink.

Knowing your limitations and those of your guests will help you be responsible. As a host, don't urge a drink on someone who refuses. If you're a guest who's been told to avoid alcohol, do so. Don't put your host on the spot. Making a "one-drink" exception could be hazardous. You'll find plenty of nonalcoholic drinks to quench your thirst and lift your spirits.

In this chapter, you'll learn how alcohol works in your system. You'll see why it's so important to pace yourself when you drink. You'll read how you can enjoy an occasional drink and still lose weight. And, if you don't pay attention and use some caution, you'll read what you can do to ease that splitting hangover headache.

When you toast, "to your health," you'll mean it.

CHEERS FOR RESPONSIBLE DRINKING

Drinking is a festive, social activity. Reading about health and safety concerns related to alcohol is such a downer you may be tempted to turn the page. Unfortunately, ignoring the possible consequences of drinking won't make them vanish. If you inadvertently cause an accident because you've served too much liquor at a party or cause a health crisis by serving liquor to a guest who shouldn't be drinking, you'll carry the burden of guilt and possible legal action as well.

You can avoid this by taking some necessary steps. First, learn how your body uses alcohol.

It's True—Alcohol Can be Deadly!

Most people begin to show signs of mental impairment at 0.05 percent BAL. At 0.10 percent, people start to stagger; at 0.15 percent, they begin to slur their speech. If they reach a blood alcohol level of 0.3 percent, they may pass out. Above 0.4 results in a coma, and at 0.5 percent BAL, their hearts may stop beating and they stop breathing. All this can happen in a single binge episode. One night of heavy alcohol consumption could end in death.

The One-Minute Biology Course

Alcohol is a drug that acts in contrasting ways. You've heard people say they "feel no pain" when they've had a drink or two. Alcohol can desensitize you. Yet it also stimulates you to do things that aren't sensible. If you have a little too much to drink, you may be less inhibited. You'll say and do things you wouldn't dare were you sober. These effects can be triggered soon after you start drinking. Many factors influence alcohol's impact.

Let's start with a short lesson on how your body absorbs alcohol. As soon as you take a drink, your body starts pumping alcohol into your bloodstream. Unlike food that can take hours to digest, alcohol moves swiftly into your system. Food slows the absorption of alcohol by competing for first rights into your system.

According to one study, people who drink alcohol after a meal that contains fat, protein, and carbohydrates absorbed alcohol about three times more slowly than when they consumed alcohol on an empty stomach.

If you hear about people who are arrested for "driving under the influence," you'll hear the term BAC for blood alcohol concentration or BAL for blood alcohol level. Both are

The Breathalyzer

Your body digests most of the alcohol you consume. A small portion is excreted, unchanged, through your breath. That's what police measure if you receive a breath alcohol test.

a measure of alcohol in the body. That's what law enforcement officials look at. Acceptable BAC or BAL maximums vary among the states.

Your BAC is determined by whether you're drinking on a full or empty stomach; how much you drink; the percent of alcohol in your drink; your age, weight, and sex; and the rate at which you eliminate the liquid.

The more you drink and the higher the proof (the percent of alcohol), the higher your BAC will be. If you have a slight build, you'll have a higher BAC than if you're a large person. Men, it's true, can hold their liquor better than women. Women can blame their smaller size, greater percentage of body fat, and lower percentage of body water for higher BAC scores.

For normal drinking, such as cocktails after work, your highest BAC usually occurs within thirty minutes of polishing off the drink. It could take up to sixty minutes for your body to register its highest BAC. However, if you drink large quantities of alcohol, or eat a large meal while you consume alcohol, your body may continue to absorb the alcohol for another two hours. Have two Martinis followed by a steak dinner, and you may feel fine, but your BAC may still be hitting its peak, which means you could be a danger to someone.

Your body metabolizes alcohol at a much slower rate than it absorbs it. Remember, it takes only thirty to sixty minutes before the spirits hit your bloodstream. But your

BAC will decrease at a rate of about 15 percent an hour. Cold showers, coffee, or walks won't speed this up.

THE RESPONSIBLE IMBIBER

Now that you know how lingering alcohol's effects are, you'll want to serve and order drinks judiciously.

- Never give anyone more than one drink an hour. Experts recommend not consuming more than three drinks in a day; limiting consumption to two drinks a day is preferable. If your guest got a head start somewhere else, include that in your calculations.
- If a guest is making frequent visits to the bar, distract him or her with food or nonalcoholic drinks.
- Always supply food at a cocktail party. Your food arrangement could be a simple assortment of cheeses, vegetables roasted in olive oil, and whole-grain breads. Skip salty chips and nuts or you'll make your guests thirsty.
- If you're going to a party and don't have time for a meal, eat a peanut butter sandwich, which supplies protein and fat.
- Always have nonalcoholic beverages on hand. An hour before your party is scheduled to end, switch to serving nonintoxicating drinks.

Be Prepared

You may encounter special situations at parties. Knowing how to respond beforehand will alleviate many potential problems:

- Never offer or serve alcohol to a minor.
- Never serve alcohol to a woman who is pregnant. If, as a guest, you are a woman trying to get pregnant, skip alcohol. You may already be pregnant. Any alcohol in the first trimester could seriously harm your baby.

The DUI

DUI, driving under the influence (of alcohol), or DWI, driving while intoxicated, are two terms you don't want to become intimately familiar with. Limits for blood alcohol concentration are set at the state level. If you want to know what your state defines as DUI or DWI, check with the appropriate state agency. (Or, using an Internet search engine, type in your state and "driver alcohol limits" and you'll find the information.)

- If you're taking any medications, ask your physician or pharmacist whether you should avoid alcohol. Don't give an alcoholic drink to someone you know is on medication unless you know it's safe.
- Be cautious in offering alcoholic beverages to seniors who may have problems with balance.
- Just as you know not to give a drink to someone who's going to be driving a car, be equally aware and don't serve alcohol to swimmers (especially at a lake or ocean that might have an undertow), boaters, skiers, or snowmobilers.

Saying No

Despite your best efforts, you've got an insistent buddy who won't take no for an answer. He'll argue that the amount he's consuming is his responsibility; you're not his mother, wife, or partner; he can handle it and he won't forgive you if you don't give him another drink. Take a deep breath and offer this line: "No, I won't give you a drink because I like you too much."

It usually works when all else fails. What possible argument can someone offer to that?

Medicine Danger!

Whatever you do, don't chase a painkiller with an alcoholic drink. Some combinations of painkillers—even nonprescription ones—and alcohol are so caustic to your stomach they can cause bleeding. Wait until alcohol leaves your system, usually by the next morning, before you take a medication. More potent painkillers could prove toxic when mixed with alcohol.

 ## COLLEGE DRINKING

Drinking in college is a rite of passage, like dorm parties or post-football bashes. Yet excessive drinking in school can have such dire consequences, you need to be aware of the damage you or a loved one may be suffering from this behavior.

Binge drinking, which is lining up and shooting down at least five drinks in a row for men or four drinks in a row for women, can lead to alcohol poisoning, accidents, and destructive behavior. If you think binge drinking isn't happening among your friends or to your college-age children, think again. According to the Harvard School of Public Health's 1999 College Alcohol Study, more than 40 percent of college students admitted to binge drinking at least once in the two weeks preceding the data collection.

Binge drinkers are more likely to be hurt or killed in car accidents or swimming mishaps; they're more likely to have poor class attendance and failing grades.

Being drunk and out of control puts young people at greater risk of having unprotected sex and acquiring sexually transmitted diseases. Young women who binge drink are vulnerable to date rape.

When drunk, students pose a nuisance or danger to others. They need help taking care of themselves, they get into fights, and they're generally obnoxious to be around.

Many schools are taking steps, such as counseling or peer group monitoring, to reduce binge drinking. However, students can make some healthy changes as well:

- Learn alternatives to alcohol for unwinding. Doing de-stressing techniques, such as meditation or exercising, are two proven choices.
- Don't hang around students who are heavy drinkers.
- Find structured activities for weekends. Go to a play or a movie with friends instead of hitting the bars.
- Realize there's nothing sexy or glamorous about being drunk.

HANGOVER HEADACHES

No doubt you're a sensible drinker (otherwise you wouldn't be reading this). However, you may suffer the occasional hangover—your head feels like it's in a vise, your stomach is on its own roller-coaster ride, and your eyeballs are screaming for relief.

There are several villains you can blame for your misery. Consider all the things you're ingesting—sulfites, herbs, ethanol, sugars—and it's no wonder your head might reel. Chemical impurities that give drinks their distinctive taste, color, and aroma are called "congeners." They can add up to a mighty hangover. It's unfortunate, but the more flavorful the product, the more congeners it has. Red wine, brandy, and whiskey rank high for congeners, as does dark rum. Vodka, which is odorless and colorless, has few.

In addition to impurities, you're getting a diuretic—the ethanol in alcohol—which can leave you reeling. You void more liquid than you take in and your brain sends out an alarm when it starts to lose too much water. That's the blasted ringing in your head. Also, the more you urinate, the

How Much Alcohol Is Too Much?

You know the drill:

- You drink more than you planned.
- You drink even though your friends and family urge you to cut back.
- You can't wait to have a drink.
- You have to drink more alcohol each time to get that "good" feeling.

If you relate to any of the above, seek professional help. You don't have to drink alcoholic beverages to have a pleasurable time at gatherings.

more you're voiding essential sodium and potassium in your system. The imbalance gives you a headache. And, when your body digests alcohol it releases free radicals, which act as toxins, in the process. No wonder you don't feel good.

However, there are some things you can do to alleviate the symptoms.

Cures

The popular advice is to avoid caffeine when you've got a hangover. The reasoning is that liquor dehydrated you, and coffee will lead to further dehydration, exacerbating your misery.

Not so, say researchers at the Center for Human Nutrition in Omaha, Nebraska, who issued a press release on the results of their experiments. They put eighteen men in their twenties and thirties on various fluid regimens— water, caffeinated soft drinks, and coffee—then measured their urine output and blood to check their levels of hydration. The choice of beverage did not affect their output.

The only exception might be for people who usually don't drink coffee. The researchers say that the body adapts to caffeine over time.

With the caffeine issue out of the way, you can try a cup of coffee as your first defense. Caffeine is known to prevent blood vessels from dilating and causing pain.

You can also try foods or drinks that contain fructose, found in fruit juice and honey. Fructose may help your body burn alcohol faster, according to the National Institutes of Health, a division of the U.S. government. One soothing way to get fructose—and caffeine—is in tea with honey.

You should drink plenty of water to prevent dehydration. Also sip some bouillon to replace the salt and eat a banana to supply the potassium you lost by drinking alcohol.

Avoiding Hangovers

After your first hangover, you'll undoubtedly say, "Never again." Here are some steps you can take to lessen the chance of another painful morning.

- Drink slowly and on a full stomach. Before drinking, eat a peanut butter sandwich on whole wheat bread for fat, protein, and complex carbohydrates.
- There are a number of theories on what you should or should not drink to avoid a hangover. For example, although there's no scientific evidence for it, some people suggest that you not mix grain and grape. Other advice is to avoid liqueurs on the theory that the high sugar content gives you a headache.
- Avoid alcoholic beverages that are high in congeners. Also opt for better brands, which have fewer impurities.
- Drink plenty of water.

 # DRINKING AND DIETING

Years ago, when steaks and Martinis were as obligatory as cars with fins, people didn't question whether booze was fattening. This was long before health was on peoples' minds; back then, water was the only noncaloric beverage most people drank.

Drinkers who associated liquor with weight gain were re-assured that there was no connection. Witness the popular-ity of the "drinking man's diet," in the mid 1960s, which suggested you could have your drinks and your svelte fig-ure, too.

So much more is known about nutrition now. And it's well-established that alcohol has calories. However, you can enjoy alcohol and maintain your current weight or even lose weight.

Like any food or beverage with calories, alcohol will make you fat if you consume more calories than you burn. You can budget for drink calories if you cut back elsewhere. For example, have one Martini, but skip the chips. You can also increase your exercise. Have that Screwdriver, but get on the treadmill for an hour.

You may also be at risk for weight gain if you lose your willpower when you drink, and eat more than you should. Below you'll find tips for dealing with the munchies.

How caloric is alcohol? One ounce—that's two table-spoons—of liquor has from 65 to 83 calories. The greater the proof, the more calories the product has. For example, 1 ounce of 80-proof liquor has 65 calories, 1 ounce of 86-proof liquor has 70 calories, 1 ounce of 90-proof has 74 calo-ries, 1 ounce of 94-proof has 77 calories, and 1 ounce of 100-proof liquor has 83 calories.

You're also getting calories in most mixers. A 6-ounce glass of orange juice has 83 calories. Yes, it also has vitamin C, which is very good for you, but this is a diet conversation. Take a cola for 75 to 85 calories or tonic water at 65 calories for 6 ounces. Add the 130 calories in a two-ounce serving of gin with 65 calories for the tonic and you've got a 195-calorie drink. Down a couple of cream-and-coffee-liqueur combos and you may be getting 500 calories more than you anticipated. This could lead to a weight problem.

Tips for the Svelte

You have some options. If you're concerned about your weight, try one of these solutions:

- Opt for one, not three cocktails at a party. When you've had your drink, switch to diet tonic water with a squeeze of lime and party on.
- Use diet versions instead of caloric tonic water for Gin and Tonics.
- Add less sugar to Whiskey Sours.
- Don't ask for your drink on-the-rocks. You're likely to go for seconds. Instead, cut drinks with water or club soda. You'll be satisfied with less.
- Switch to a less-fattening drink, such as a White Wine Spritzer, coming in at less than 50 calories a serving. (You'll find the recipe in chapter 6.)

If your appetite-control center goes on hold whenever you drink, make some adjustments. Before a party, do one of the following:

- Eat a light meal to dull your appetite.
- Load your plate with fruits and vegetables so you feel full on fewer calories.
- Don't stand in front of the hors d'oeuvre table. Get out, mingle, talk to people. It's hard to talk with your mouth full.

 # THE LAST WORD

Every day, you hear or read something about alcohol and your health, and it's as likely as not that the information contradicts what you heard before. Is a drink a day good for you? Or could that drink be linked to health concerns in the future?

The reason you're getting conflicting reports is that the even the experts aren't sure about the answers yet. Much depends on your overall health. The information may also depend on what disease you're trying to prevent.

For instance, a drink a day, or less, may help you avoid heart disease. Alcohol has been shown to reduce the narrowing of arteries, increase your body's "good cholesterol" (HDL-cholesterol), and lower your risk of blood clots.

Don't worry if you don't drink. There are plenty of other ways, such as reducing stress, increasing exercise, and eating a diet high in fruits and vegetables and low in saturated fat, that will lower your chances of developing heart disease. Although alcohol is heart protective, it may increase your risk of developing cancer of the mouth or breast cancer, if you're a woman. (There's not much research suggesting whether or not alcohol is linked to breast cancer in men.) In addition, the relationship of alcohol to cancer is dose-dependent. The more you drink, the greater your chance of developing breast or certain other cancers.

As a potentially beneficial beverage, medical researchers debate whether any alcohol will do or whether wine, because of its specific chemical components, is more healthful. Some scientists feel it's not really the alcohol that's helpful, but the fact that people who drink in moderation are more likely to eat a healthful diet and get plenty of exercise.

Stay tuned for more definitive recommendations. Until then, you'll want to follow the agreed-upon advice and stick to no more than moderate drinking, which is defined as one drink a day for adult women or two drinks a day for adult men. One drink is defined as 1.5 ounces of 80-proof liquor (about what you'd get in a weak Gin and Tonic), 12 ounces of beer, or 5 ounces of wine.

If you're a woman you should be especially cautious. As a woman, you process alcohol differently than men do, and tend to accumulate more alcohol in your body. That's because you have lower levels of stomach enzymes that neutralize alcohol before it moves into your bloodstream. You also have a higher proportion of body fat (yes, despite those killer crunches) that does not absorb alcohol, leaving it to flow into the blood. Finally, you most likely weigh less than a man so you're taking in a higher proportion of alcohol per body weight than a man is.

And if you are pregnant or are trying to conceive, you should not drink, say medical experts. There is no safe level of alcoholic intake. Women who drink as few as one or two drinks a day during pregnancy may miscarry or give birth to premature babies or babies with neurological problems, according to the *Harvard Medical School Family Health Guide* (Simon & Schuster, 1999).

8

Ay Caramba!

It's Party Time

If you've been following this book from the beginning, you've stocked your bar, wiped the spots from your glasses, and bought a monster of an ice-crushing blender. You make a perfect Manhattan and a stellar Cosmopolitan. So why aren't you writing out your guest list? As the rocker Reverend Horton Heat says, "It's Martini time!" You know how to make that killer cocktail and a couple dozen more. Share those dazzling drinks with your friends. Pay people back for their invitations, break the ice with new acquaintances, or just kick back and have fun.

If you've never hosted a cocktail party, you're probably feeling a combination of excitement and anxiety. That's understandable. Some party guides scold you if your napkins don't match or if you haven't carved place cards from blocks of aged Parmesan. Good grief! You don't know if you're playing host to a few pals or the secretary of protocol for the United Nations. Fortunately, this book won't grade you on your party savvy.

Instead, you can use *The Absolute Beginner's Guide* as a resource that holds the keys to becoming a gracious host.

You'll learn how to throw a fabulous cocktail party, starting with invitations that put your guests in a state of eager anticipation. You'll set up your bar like a pro. What's more, you'll prepare delightful morsels that complement your cocktails. And you'll dazzle your guests with sociability that sends a jolt of electricity through a room.

But maybe you've always hated a crowd scene. You turn as green as a Daiquiri when faced with a room full of people. Check the "Cocktails and . . ." section of this chapter. There you'll find comfortable alternatives to a bash.

Did you ever imagine people wanting to crash your parties? They will. Let's start.

> ### Helpful Hint
> Your guests will arrive in thirty minutes and you forgot to chill the champagne for Mimosas. What do you do? Place the champagne in a large bucket and alternately pack in layers of salt and ice. Salt lowers the freezing point of ice, causing it to melt. In the process, ice takes heat energy from the champagne, cooling it.

 ## THE COCKTAIL PARTY

It builds up like an uncontrollable urge and before you know it, you've got to have a party.

You're going to have so much fun—honest! And the more organized you are, the less nervous you'll be and the more time you'll have to enjoy your company because you won't be flitting around troubleshooting little emergencies.

Take the time to think through all the steps to party giving. If you've sent out invitations well in advance, ordered your supplies, and hired any help you need, you'll be relaxed and calm when the first guest comes through the door. You'll learn everything there is to know to be a great host or hostess in this chapter.

What's Your Theme?

Although you don't need an excuse to have a party, it can be useful to have a theme. The right theme can inspire the design of your invitations, your drinks, your menu, and your decorations. Themes can be kitschy, knock-you-over-the-head silly, or very adult. If, however, you prefer a minimalist approach, you'll find that a little candlelight, a vase of flowers, and a stack of CDs provide all the atmosphere you need.

Holidays are a great stimulus. You get built-in themes with menus that are obviously appropriate. For example, start your creative juices flowing as you plan a spooktail celebration for Halloween. Tell your friends to dress in their bewitching best. Decorate your home with strings of orange lights and cardboard cats. Set up a coffin cooler for beer and soft drinks. Place a bowl of punch on a tray of dry ice. Drizzle water on the dry ice for a fog effect. Serve finger sandwiches as your hors d'oeuvre. And don't forget a Bloody Mary; this is her holiday. Hey, you don't have to be a twelve-year-old to have Halloween fun.

If you're not a football fan, you may not realize half of America stops functioning on Super Bowl Sunday. Sports jock or not, you can join them for Sangria or Bullshots, a combination of vodka and beef broth. Add a few appetizers for halftime and you're an instant sports hero.

Valentine's Day calls for especially seductive ploys. Invite one person for Champagne Cocktails or have a crowd over for Cosmopolitans.

Or go farther afield in your celebrations. Check the Internet. You'll find plenty of commemorations that demand

> **Fun Fact!**
>
> The longest recorded flight of a popped champagne cork was 177 feet and 9 inches. The low-flying cork was launched at Woodbury Vineyards in New York State.

your attention. You can't let National Watermelon Day (last year it was August 3) go by without notice. Send out green watermelon-shaped invitations. Include a few watermelon seeds in the envelope, which guests may redeem for a special Watermelon Margarita or a Watermelon Cooler (see chapter 6). This author's favorite is August 25, Kiss and Make Up Day. Oooh, what a party image that day conjures up.

The Guest List

Visualize your living room filled with people. How many can you squeeze in before feet no longer touch the floor? That's the maximum number of guests you'll invite. Reduce the list if:

> ## Helpful Hint
>
> It's nearly impossible to squeeze a cork back into a champagne bottle. Once released, champagne corks puff out like sponges. You can buy champagne stoppers in many liquor stores. Other options: save used wine corks to seal champagne or shop in a science supply house for test-tube corks; both work well to seal in bubbles. Finish half-full bottles of champagne within a day or two.

- You're on a budget.
- Your lease limits how many people you can bring in.
- You want to get to know that cute coworker.

Speaking of coworkers, don't bring your office home with you. Mix up your guest list. Get to know new people. Nothing is worse than office talk, and the same old conversations after three Martinis become excruciating. Do, however, invite your pal who's a charming conversationalist. You need one ice-breaking guest in any soiree.

Avoid:

- Children. Discourage your friends from bringing theirs and hide yours in the attic with a Game Boy.

- Guests who share the same career. A room full of lawyers, doctors, or journalists is instant novocaine.
- Couples who are breaking up or former partners in a relationship.
- Anyone who has been on any of the following TV shows: *Survivor, Temptation Island,* or *Big Brother.*

Defining Your Party

"Cocktails" or "cocktail party" means your guests will stand around sipping and nibbling. Attire can be casual or business. The term "cocktail buffet" says you're offering enough food for a light dinner and a spot to sit down and eat. "Cocktail reception" is a pull-out-the-stops occasion. It's usually a catered party in which the food and champagne flow. And it's usually dressy. Wedding celebrations, for example, call for cocktail receptions. And finally, there's the "Cocktails and . . ." alternative (in this chapter), for those who aren't quite ready to deal with a full-blown cocktail party.

 # THE INVITATIONS

I still believe in written invitations for several reasons:

- You can set a theme that your guests will eagerly embrace.
- Guests are less likely to misunderstand or forget the directions: "I thought the party started at eight." "No. It ends at eight. Look at your invitation."
- You're more likely to give guests information you might otherwise forget.
- It makes your party special. You're setting a tone that says, "This is more than an evening watching a video."

Adult party invitations should be straightforward, not cute. Include the following in your message:

- Date and beginning and ending times. The stretch between 5 and 8 P.M. is the most popular for cocktail parties.

- RSVP information. You'll want to get a head count.
- The theme if there is one.
- Name of guest of honor, if appropriate.
- Some cue as to dress code: casual, informal, come-as-you-are, semiformal, or formal.
- Directions, if necessary.
- Parking suggestions.

Your casual invitation may be similar to this:

Bev Bennett invites you to share cocktails and good cheer to break in her newly installed bar.
Sunday evening,
April first
From four to seven
123 Fourth Street
Anywhere City
RSVP 123-4567
Casual dress

Or . . . your formal invitation may read something like this:

Ms. Bev Bennett requests the pleasure of your company
at a cocktail party to celebrate the invention of the Cosmopolitan
Friday evening, April first
From five to eight
123 Fourth Street
Anywhere City
RSVP 123-4567   *Black Tie*

Note: If neighborhood parking is nonexistent or you live in a hard-to-find area, insert a second page with useful

Fun Fact!

Historically, the Camba Indians of Eastern Bolivia were notorious for their excessive alcohol consumption. Their liquor of choice was a distillate of sugarcane that produced a 178-proof spirit. The Camba males drank this in enormous amounts. The potent drink brought tears to the eyes of even seasoned drinkers, and drove the population into days of drunken stupor. The habitual drinking declined during the 1960s when the natives found other ways for community bonding.

information, regardless of the type of invitation you issue. You do want guests to arrive unruffled.

Don't be afraid of dress-up parties. People may kvetch about silks and stockings, but they secretly love putting on finery they otherwise have no excuse to wear. Watch how people behave when they're in their best attire. You may see a new side of your friends.

Mail your invitations at least three weeks before your event, four weeks in advance during the fall-winter holiday season.

PLANNING STRATEGIES

Take stock of your resources before you begin your party plans. Make sure you either have, or can get, the supplies you need. Also, decide how much you want to take on. You don't want to be stressed or exhausted when company comes. You may decide to scale back your plans or to hire some help. Before you send out your invitations, ask yourself the following questions:

- **Do I have enough glasses?**

  Assume everyone will use two glasses. Either they'll misplace one glass or they'll switch drinks. Have available two glasses per person. You don't need to buy new glasses. But if you're ready to give up the highball glasses with the gas station logo, this author won't object. Expect to pay from $2 to $10 per glass for replacements.

  For larger parties (fifteen to fifty guests), you may want to use good-quality plastic cups instead of glassware. Look for cups that don't buckle when filled with liquid. Plastic cups come in a variety of shapes. You're likely to find plastic versions of wine, highball, or cocktail glasses. Plastic will run you 10 to 50 cents each.

For fifty or more guests, rentals may be your best bet. Glasses go for 30 to 40 cents. Ask whether delivery and pick-up fees are included or extra. You may be able to negotiate.

About three-fourths of your glassware should be highballs, and the remainder lowballs. Highballs are more popular. Don't forget to order flutes if you're serving champagne.

- **How about dishes?**
If you plan on serving any wet food—meatballs and gravy, fondue, red peppers vinaigrette—use ceramic dishes. You can rent them along with the glasses.

Good-quality paper plates are fine for Endive Bites or Curried, Candied Walnuts (see chapter 10), or other foods that won't turn plates soggy.

- **What about cooking and storing food?**
You'll be pleased to see how easy it is to make delicious appetizers using the recipes in this book. But if you don't have refrigerator or freezer space, you may want to trim your menu or borrow refrigerator space from a neighbor.

Fun Fact!

A "neat" drink is alcohol poured right from the bottle into a glass that doesn't contain ice. A "straight-up" drink is poured into a glass with ice so that it chills. Then it's strained and poured into a second glass without ice.

- **Who's going to play bartender?**
Don't you want to be the bottle jockey? You'll enjoy bartending more if you aren't overwhelmed. Tell your

guests you have three or four drinks on the menu. Limit choices or offer pitcher drinks as an alternative.

For more than fifty guests, however, call in the pros. You'll be paying anywhere from $75 to $125 for three hours, plus gratuity. Ask a professional if he or she is supplying equipment and glassware. Some do, which will save you having to rent glasses. You may hire an amateur for about $15 an hour, but make sure this person is over twenty-one.

- **Are you going to clean your house or get someone else to do it?**

A professional cleaning team, running through your house like a cyclone, will get your party ready in two hours or less and charge $150 to $250. A private individual will do the job in eight hours with a fee of $10 to $15 per hour. You can also hire someone for $10 to $15 per hour to manage the mess during your party.

> ### Helpful Hint
> When tending bar, simple syrup is easier to use if you make a large batch and pour it into a clean bottle topped with a speed pourer.

Three to Four Weeks in Advance

- Send out invitations.
- Reserve any necessary equipment, including glassware. Rent or borrow dishes and glassware if necessary.
- Hire any cleaning and bartending help. If you're scheduling a party during the Thanksgiving through New Year holiday season, you should hire your wait staff at least three months ahead. Look for last-minute help at your local college. Call the placement counselor. Set up a face-to-face meeting with amateur hires. Remember you're not going to get trained butlers, so be specific about your needs. Write lists in advance of what you'll expect from your unskilled, but eager help.

Five Absolutely Unbreakable Rules for Successful Cocktail Party Giving

1. Have fewer chairs than you have guests. One chair for every three people is about right, or two clusters of three to four chairs for a gathering of twenty.

2. Choose the music yourself. You'll never know when someone will discover that Frank Yankovic recording of "Who Stole the Kiska" you thought you tossed out years ago.

3. Keep the food coming. If you're going to find it difficult to break away during your party, ask or hire someone else to refill the trays so you don't have to.

4. Have a secret buddy. This isn't an official host, but your best asset. She has eyes in the back of her head, can arrange food on a tray in less than thirty seconds, and can get a wine stain out of white linen.

5. Discourage your guests from lingering past party time. Your guests will notice that you've closed the booze bottles and stopped replenishing the food trays. If that doesn't get people reaching for their coats, you can start clearing glasses. Finally, if you've got a devoted, fun-loving crowd, enlist a friend. Your pal can look at his watch and say, "It's getting late; time to go." If you're too cowardly to chase them out at the appointed time, give someone else the dirty job.

Two to Three Weeks in Advance

- Plan the food. Finding the recipes you'll want to serve is as easy as flipping the pages of this book. Buy nonperishable ingredients.

- Stock up on spirits. When you shop ahead you can look for bargains. Use the shopping section of this chapter to write your list.

- Eliminate any eyesores. Throw out those moth-eaten towels and get new ones, now. Splurge on a set of cool napkins from your favorite store.
- Make and freeze foods. Check the tips in chapter 10. You'll see plenty of hints for advance preparations along with the recipes.
- Pinch pennies if you have to—wear last year's sequin-studded top or serve the store brand of club soda—but hire and schedule someone to clean your house the day before your party. You will be so much calmer knowing someone caught all the dust bunnies.
- If table linens need cleaning, drop them off at the dry cleaner.
- Either get carpets and upholstered furniture profes-sionally cleaned, or stock up on black light bulbs.

Three to Five Days in Advance

- Decide what you're going to wear . . . and stick with it. I recall one party during my uncertain sartorial days when I was tearing my way through the closet until the doorbell rang. I finally emerged but didn't notice until halfway through the evening that my mascara was smudged and I was wearing one black and one brown shoe.
- Grocery shop for perishable foods, including lemons and limes for garnishes.
- Have any rental equipment delivered.
- Call any guests who didn't RSVP.

Two or Three Days in Advance

- Buy lots of flowers. Select open buds if it's just before party day, and partially closed buds if you have a couple of days to spare.
- Call your wait staff. Make sure they know everything they're supposed to do.
- Decorate. If you have a theme, make sure you have dishes, fabrics, flowers, and music to match.

Songs for a Sentimental Mood

Shop in any record store or even many lifestyle stores and you'll find CDs "for cocktail parties." To this author's sensibilities, buying premixed cocktail music is like buying canned drinks. You'll get a pasteurized selection. Instead, choose music—from ambient-techno-jazz to Frank Sinatra—to suit your own taste.

Here are ten musical selections that get my parties off to a good start:

"Saturday Night" from the musical *Company* by Stephen Sondheim

"Not a Day Goes By" from the musical *Merrily We Roll Along* by Stephen Sondheim

"Brother Can You Spare a Dime" sung by Mandy Patinkin

"Young at Heart" sung by Frank Sinatra

"Harlem Nocturne" by Earle Hogel

"Piano Man" sung by Billy Joel

"Because I Got High" sung by Afroman

"Mercy, Mercy Me" sung by Marvin Gaye

Under the Table and Dreaming, CD, the Dave Matthews Band

Billie Holiday's Greatest Hits, CD, sung by Billie Holiday

One Day in Advance

- Don't panic.
- Clean your bathroom. Put out clean towels, new bars of soap, and a bottle of hand lotion. Place a vase of flowers in the bathroom.
- Set up a collapsible coat rack in a convenient spot in the hall or a bedroom.

- Arrange a few chairs in conversational groupings.
- Set out the CDs you'll want to play.
- Stop cooking. What, you say? You've still got all kinds of food to make. OK, you can make a few odds and ends, but garlic and Gershwin don't mix. It will take about four hours to get rid of lingering onion and garlic smells. Aromatic foods should be made well in advance.
- Take out the garbage, especially in the kitchen and bathroom.
- Set up your food table. Include tableware, napkins, and serving pieces. Place a serving dish on the table for every food you'll serve. Place a note in each dish indicating what food goes in it. An hour before the party you won't wonder in what you're serving the Shrimp with Mustard Sauce.

> ### Helpful Hint
> Be sure to ice a six-pack or two. Beer is still the most popular alcoholic beverage in the United States.

- Set up the bar (details follow). Include everything that doesn't need refrigeration such as glasses, napkins, and utensils.
- Put floral arrangements in your party room, your kitchen, and bedroom. Fill the house with scents.
- If necessary, change the lightbulbs for a soft glow.
- Set out a couple of garbage cans in the kitchen and one next to the bar.
- Cut lemons and limes into slices, wedges, and twists. Place lemons and limes in separate plastic bags and squeeze out excess air. Refrigerate.
- By now you've moved your frozen party food to the refrigerator. Stock your freezer with ice cubes and crushed ice.
- Take a look at your party room just before you go to bed. It looks so fabulous you can't wait until your friends come.

 # SHOPPING

Correctly estimating how much your guests will eat or drink is about as tricky as predicting the next winning season for the Chicago Cubs. There are so many variables:

- Your fabulous drinks may tempt guests to consume more than you expected.
- The newest Internet diet says you'll melt pounds away with tequila. Naturally everyone wants to try that one.
- Everyone is talking, drinking, having fun, and getting carried away.

Revel in the good cheer your party generates, but take a peek at chapter 7 to see health and safety recommendations for alcohol consumption. As a general rule, restrict service to one alcoholic drink per person per hour. Guests will consume three drinks at most during a three-hour party.

If you're a math whiz or just love to do puzzles, whip out the calculator and use these guidelines to determine your shopping list (if you're not, see alternative method below):

- Most hard-liquor drinks in *The Absolute Beginner's Guide* call for 1½ to 2 ounces of a spirit; you'll get about

---

Helpful Hint

During the warm-weather months, people order more drinks with light-colored alcohol; during cold weather they switch to brown liquors. Young guests (over age twenty-one, of course) usually prefer light drinks and are more interested in sweet-tasting cocktails or more elaborate concoctions. Older guests are more likely to want brown drinks, such as whiskey or scotch, straight up.

twelve to sixteen servings from one 750-milliliter bottle.

- A straight serving of wine or champagne is 5 ounces. You'll get five servings from a 750-milliliter bottle. If you mix wine with other ingredients and only serve 4 ounces, you'll get six servings per bottle.

If you share this author's math phobia and numbers greater than ten make your eyes glaze over, here's a grocery list designed to ensure that you have more than enough liquor to satisfy your guests and eliminate your anxieties.

For Ten to Twenty Guests

2 to 3 liters vodka
2 liters gin
2 liters rum
1 to 2 liters tequila
1 liter whiskey
1 liter bourbon
1 liter scotch
1 liter brandy
½ liter each dry and sweet vermouth
6 bottles wine (half red and half white or according to your taste)

Helpful Hint

For a brunch party, you'll want to stock ingredients for lighter cocktails than for an evening one. For a morning event, champagne, orange juice, tomato juice, and vodka may be sufficient for a pleasing menu of Champagne Cocktails, Screwdrivers, and Bloody Marys.

You'll need mixers and soft drinks in addition to alcoholic beverages. For ten to twenty guests add the following to your grocery cart: Two liters (or quarts) of mixer for every liter of alcohol you buy. For example, if you pick up a liter of vodka, buy two liters of tonic water or a liter of tonic and a liter of tomato juice. Buy at least one liter of soft drinks—a combination of diet and regular—for every two guests. Purchase more nonalcoholic beverages if your guests don't consume much alcohol.

If you've ever been on an ice run in the middle of a party, it's a good way to ruin your night. For ten to twenty guests, purchase twenty pounds of ice. Five pounds of that should be crushed ice. And just so you don't have to cut olives into wedges to have enough to go around, pick up the following drink garnishes for ten to twenty guests:

5 lemons
5 limes
1 jar pimiento-stuffed olives (about 16 ounces)
1 jar cocktail onions (about 8 ounces)

LOCATION, LOCATION, LOCATION: ARRANGING YOUR BAR AND FOOD TABLES

Think of the bar and the food tables as the collective heart of your party. To keep this heart beating, people have to circulate between the two. Put the food and bar on separate tables in opposite sides of the room so that people are forced to walk back and forth. If you have a large crowd, divide the food between two tables so that one spot in the room doesn't become congested.

For a small casual group, place your liquor, mixers, a bucket of ice, tongs, glassware, and garnishes on a cart, roll it into the party room, and either take orders or suggest your specialties.

For a large party in which you star as bartender, set up a professional-looking bar. You'll want to arrange liquor, garnishes, ice, and glassware in some logical order that allows you to mix drinks quickly; haphazard displays could lead to disaster. Imagine some dishy guy or gal is asking you to make an Old-Fashioned with a twist of lemon. You rummage around for a paring knife. No luck. You abruptly end your flirtation to run into the kitchen for a knife when you could have been asking for a phone number. Don't let that happen to you. Organize!

> ## Helpful Hint
>
> When Realtors want to sell a house, they fill it with a homey, inviting scent. Their trick: put a pot of apple cider mixed with a couple of cinnamon sticks and cloves on the stove and allow to simmer for an hour or two. Try it during the fall. Your apartment will smell like apple pie. Likewise, citrus scents are summer pleasers. Fill bowls with lemons and limes. Roll fruit on the counter first to release the aromas.

Choose a large, sturdy table. You can buy or rent a folding table of the appropriate height from a rental company. Your table should come up to your mid-waist so you don't have to bend and stretch to reach your supplies. A two-tiered table allows you to keep the liquor bottles near you and the napkins on a ledge where guests can help themselves. Cover the table with a dark-colored cotton-polyester cloth that's washable and doesn't show stains.

Arrange your utensils in a row closest to you. Include your corkscrew, paring knife, cutting board, shaker, spoons, and whatever else you need. Place highball glasses on one side of the utensils and lowball glasses on the other side. If you're going to make blended drinks, make sure your table is near an electrical outlet. The blender's cord should be long enough to drop to the floor. Place the blender on the left or right end of this first row. If you're not using a blender, add an ice bucket to this row. Add a second bucket with crushed ice if you think you'll need it.

Jell Shooters

It jiggles and wiggles and tickles inside you as the child-hood rhyme goes. But this is no toddler treat. It's a Jell Shooter, the snack attack and cocktail rolled into one. Start with your favorite cocktail ingredients and add gelatin.

Here's how to make a jiggler that tastes like a cherry cola with a kick:

Start with a small package of cherry gelatin and a 12-ounce can of cola. Bring 1 cup cola to boiling in a small pot. Stir in gelatin until mixture dissolves. Add remaining cold cola and ½ cup dark rum. Stir again until completely mixed. Line mini-muffin tins with small paper liners (available in supermarket baking sections). Spoon ½ ounce (1 table-spoon) of the gelatin mixture into each liner. Place in refrigerator and chill 3 hours, or until firm.

Makes 36 shooters.

In the second row, set out your garnishes, such as lemon and lime wedges, onions, and olives. Add specialty glasses to this row. If you didn't have room for ice in the first row, place it here on either end of the glasses.

The third row is for liquor. You've got a number of choices for your layout. The bottles you anticipate using most often should be within easiest reach. Some bartenders group liquors by color: clear spirits such as gin, vodka, and tequila on one side and brown spirits such as whiskey, bourbon, and brandy on the other with dry and sweet vermouth in the middle. Clear liquors are trendy, so putting them together makes sense. However, if you think you may reach for vodka when you want tequila, you may prefer to alternate light and dark bottles.

The Bartender's SAT (Savvy Alcohol Test)

Take this simple quiz to find out whether you're ready to tend bar.

1. A fifth is:
   A) A double date with one extra guy.
   B) That thing you take when you don't want to testify.
   C) A bottle of alcohol that contains 25.6 ounces of liquid. But you're more likely to find the metric equivalent, 750 milliliters.

2. A Screwdriver is:
   A) A golf club that allows you to make weird shots.
   B) A wacky person behind the wheel of a car.
   C) A highball made with vodka and orange juice.

3. A highball is:
   A) The catch that the third baseman misses.
   B) A volleyball game with intoxicated teams.
   C) A tall drink that starts with ice.

Answers: 1-C; 2-C; 3-C. If you missed one, go back to chapter 1. If you missed two or more, host a Bartender's SAT study group. Start pouring those drinks to get more practice.

Or you may arrange bottles according to your handedness. If you're left handed, for example, put the bottles you'll use most on your left.

Add one or two pitchers of water along with the liquor (use bottled, still water not carbonated water or mineral water).

Some bartenders arrange seldom-used liqueurs in a row in back of them—referred to as the "back bar." Others arrange the liqueurs and exotica in a fourth row. Include nonalcoholic mixers, fruit juices, and soft drinks in this row.

Finally, farthest from you and closest to your guests, set out stacks of napkins.

THE NAME GAME:
TRICKS TO REMEMBERING DRINKS

There are thousands of drink recipes in a mixologist's lexicon. You're not going to remember how to make every one of them. Trust this author, even the pros are stumped occasionally. Bartenders have some tricks to finesse the most popular drinks. Otherwise they'd lose a fortune in bar bets.

Look at the basic drink categories—highball, lowball or stirred, and shaken—and learn how to make four or five classic drinks in each category. For example, among the highballs, a Screwdriver is orange juice and vodka; a Bloody Mary is the one with tomato juice. Memorize these recipes. Add a Tom Collins or a Gin Fizz. Next move on to stirred drinks. Get your Martini down pat and commit a few more to memory. Then master the formulas for a few trendy drinks, such as the Cosmopolitan or the Sour Apple Martini. And don't forget what goes into the blender for Frozen Raspberry Daiquiris.

> ### Helpful Hint
> Don't spend all your time behind the bar. You don't want to be a prisoner of your own party. When no one's lined up for a drink, get out and mingle.

ONE MORE FOR THE ROAD?
THE PARTY'S OVER

It's hard to believe that "one for the road" was such a common practice. No one needs or should have a final alcoholic drink just before driving home. Instead of preparing that last drink, think of ways to turn off the spigot.

About an hour before the party ends, let people know you're serving the last round. Then, thirty minutes before your guests are scheduled to leave, pack up the bar. Discard leftover punches and pitcher drinks. Keep soft drinks and fruit juices available and encourage guests to help themselves.

Serving coffee isn't essential to ending a cocktail party, but it's a nice touch. Brew a pot of coffee and put water on to boil for tea thirty minutes before people leave. A caffeinated beverage won't make your guests sober. However, it will make people awake and alert, which may be all they need to get home.

COCKTAILS AND ...

Suppose you're not ready for a full-blown cocktail party. An ideal alternative is the "cocktails and . . ." get-together.

Cocktails and dinner
Cocktails and the theater
Cocktails and a basketball game

This type of event has several advantages:

You're creating a convivial atmosphere that will extend throughout the evening.
Your group has another destination so you don't have to feel guilty about chasing people out of your home.
You don't even have to clean the entire house. A "cocktails and . . ." party is short so people won't wander around.

Extend the invitation for an hour or two at the most. Serve drinks with a lower alcoholic content and include a menu that just takes the growl out of stomachs.

The five low-alcohol cocktails in chapter 6 are well-suited to a "cocktails and . . ." kind of party. Accompany light cocktails with a light appetizer, such as Sweet or Savory Party Twists, two of the five light appetizer recipes you'll find in chapter 10. A brief cocktail gathering featuring light food and light alcohol is just the ticket for balmy afternoons or summer nights when it's too hot to enjoy potent drinks or heavy foods.

The first time you open the door to greet your guests you may have a moment of anxiety. But once you see how much everyone is enjoying your party, you'll only wonder when to schedule the next one. Make your parties frequent and make them memorable.

9

Martinis and Manners

Party Etiquette and
Everything Else You Need to Know

Your mother taught you to say please and thank you, to never talk with your mouth full, and to never stuff yourself. However, your mom was never (at least not in her recent history) elbow-to-elbow with fifty fun-loving, Martini-sipping friends packed into a studio apartment.

Although Mom raised you to become a polite adult, she may not be able to tell you the rules of contemporary cocktail party behavior. Yet this is an aspect of etiquette you'll need to master for a successful social life. Learn what courtesies to extend and how to be a well-mannered guest or host.

Much of drink etiquette follows the good behavior you use in everyday life. For example, you pass drinks to others before taking your own. You offer to hold a drink for a guest whose hands are full.

Some rules are simply common sense. You're not going to pop champagne corks in the direction of your guests; you risk injuring someone. Likewise you're not going to leave broken glass unattended; nor are you going to fill glasses to the brim so that they overflow when your guests lift them.

Opening Champagne with Finesse

Your guests will appreciate your finesse if they don't have to duck as you release the cork from a champagne bottle. First, point that bottle away from your guests. Remove the foil wrapper and the wire "cage" that holds the cork in place. With one hand, hold the bottle at a 45-degree angle. Place a towel loosely over the cork. Gently hold the cork and the lip of the bottle with your other hand. Rotate the bottle, not the cork. As you feel the cork loosen you can ease it out using the towel.

A properly released cork will sigh, not pop.

But you'll also encounter situations for which you'll need to know the proper thing to do. Remember when you were a child and you and your friends showed up in the park on Saturday morning? Anyone who came was included in the softball game. Now you're an adult and your get-togethers are less casual.

So many questions:

Do you call to invite people over, or do you have to send a written invitation?
Do you ignore the RSVP on an invitation you receive?
Does casual dress mean jeans with holes or without?
Does semiformal mean dark suit or sport jacket?

You'll find this chapter the next best thing to having your own etiquette coach to handle drink- and party-related questions.

INVITATIONS

Unlike those college frat bashes in which invitations were spread across the campus by word-of-mouth, a cocktail party is a little more formal. After all, you're probably more discriminating and don't want to pack guests three bodies high. Send written invitations.

Sending Invitations

Include beginning and ending times. That way you won't have to resort to extreme measures to get your guests to leave. A cocktail party should clearly spell out whether guests will be fed. At your most casual, you can say something like "come for drinks" or "come for drinks and hors d'oeuvres." Don't plan your party around the dinner hour— between 6 and 8 P.M.—unless you intend to feed people substantial appetizers. Although champions of traditional etiquette might object, you may also e-mail your invitations. You'll find more party details in chapter 8.

Responding to Invitations

* Let your host know whether you're coming, and please, call sooner than the morning before the party. If the party is catered, your host has to pay for no-shows.
* Don't bring uninvited and unexpected guests. If you're attending a party of fifty or more guests, one or two more probably won't send your host into a tizzy, but ask first.
* If you have a sudden change of plans and need to cancel, let your host know as soon as possible.

DRESSING APPROPRIATELY

Check out an old movie and you'll see actresses dressed to the nines in cocktail party scenes. You'd better believe Bette Davis, as Margo Channing in *All About Eve*, wasn't sporting low-rider jeans.

More recently, no one would dare show up at a party sporting a jacket and tie or a dress. One would be labeled a "suit," a humorless bore.

Now party attire has come full circle. Some people love going glam—black dress and spiked heels. Others want the comfort of their Saturday grubbies. As a host you not only set the tone, but also must send out the message. Let your guests know what you expect them to wear.

> ## Fun Fact!
>
> English pubs serve drinks by pints or quarts. Years ago bartenders told loud, obnoxious patrons to mind their own pints and quarts, which was shortened to "Mind your Ps and Qs."

- "Come as you are" means wear whatever you like. Do cover up the essentials.
- Casual for men means sport jacket, tie optional. Casual for women includes informal pantsuits, slacks or skirts, and sweaters or blouses.
- Black tie says dress up. Men should wear a dinner jacket, white dress shirt, cummerbund, black socks, and shoes. For some black-tie events, men can get away with a dark suit with conservative shirt and tie. Women should wear short or long evening gowns with silk heels or evening sandals.

 ## BYOB?

- One sign of being a grown-up is that you no longer issue BYOB invitations. Have an assortment of alcoholic and nonalcoholic beverages available. If money is an object, you have plenty of options for meeting your budget (see chapters 2 and 6).
- You've been invited to a combination housewarming-cocktail party and you want to bring a gift of fabulous aged tequila. Dress the bottle in ribbons and explain

Serving Nondrinking Guests

As a host, you can't assume your guests want to drink alcohol. You can make nondrinkers feel at ease by offering an assortment of beverages. Create a nonalcoholic "house special" so your guests feel at ease. (See chapter 6 for tantalizing recipes.) Never urge a drink on anyone who refuses it—and never pry into someone's reason for turning down a drink.

that it's to be enjoyed some other time so the host doesn't feel obligated to open it.

- You've got champagne tastes but your host is on a beer budget. Is it okay to bring the beverage you'd rather be drinking? Nope, not unless you have enough to go round. It's rude to be sipping the "good stuff" when you don't have enough to share.

- Don't comment on the price or quality of drinks being offered. Your host is offering the best he or she can afford. You're invited to parties to enjoy yourself and to dazzle others with your charm. No grousing.

 PARTY TALK

Your first two guests arrive and stand there, staring at each other to see who blinks first. And you were expecting rousing conversation. You may need to light party fires. Do a little homework before your guests arrive so you can add a personal note to introductions: "This is John who just came from a week tracking man-eating grasshoppers in the Amazon." That should spark a lively exchange.

As your room fills and you're busy serving drinks, assign ice-breaking duties to a friend. When you're bringing together a diverse set of strangers you'll want to make sure

Mingling and Sitting It Out

Mixing is as natural as sipping a drink. However, you may have some guests who need to sit. Make sure you have chairs arranged so your guests can take a break while remaining around the action. Also be sure you don't isolate older guests who can't stand for long periods.

everyone feels comfortable. In some circles conversation topics such as sex, politics, and religion are still forbidden. Party talk would be pretty dull without a few topical jokes, but make them generic and make sure you're not offending anyone.

Don't use a cocktail party to launch a debate. If you strongly disagree with what someone is saying, change the subject or walk away. Stop tensions with a joke before they build up.

 # TOASTING

The rousing cheer to your health or that of a guest has a history as mixed as the cocktails you're drinking. To start, there are the ancient Greek and Roman religious rites of drinking to their gods and to the dead. The word "health" comes from the old English "haelth," or hail, safe and sound. Similarly "hali" is an old Scandinavian exclamation of greeting "good health to you." During Stuart times in England, drinkers put a piece of toast in their wine goblets to improve the wine's flavor. The nobles in the court of Queen Elizabeth I stood up and drank to her health. Put all the pieces together and you have toasts.

Here are some tips to ensure that toasting at your party remains the pleasant custom it should be:

Plastic or Glass, That Is the Question

Unless you throw frequent parties you probably don't have enough glassware for a crowd. Plasticware is fine for casual gatherings, such as backyard barbecues or Super Bowl parties. Paper will never do. It makes your drink taste like cardboard. Be careful if you use the cheap two-piece plastic wine or champagne glasses you have to assemble. Plastic assembled glasses fall apart easily and can make a mess for your guests.

Rent glassware for a formal party, such as your child's wedding engagement or your boss's promotion.

- Don't clang your glass to get guests' attention. Not only is it jarring, but the vibrations could cause your glass to crack or shatter. Instead, have someone circulate and quietly gather the audience.
- If you'd like someone to give a toast, ask him or her in advance. That way the designated toastmaster isn't caught by surprise.
- Don't ever embarrass, surprise, or shock the honoree with the message.
- If you've been toasted, nod and acknowledge the gesture. Do not drink. However, you should respond with a toast of your own. Then, you get to drink.

Some Toasty Toasts

A great toast separates the word-masters from the merely verbose. Raise your glass to the person you're honoring. Say something personal and meaningful, add a bit of humor and a splash of affection, and you've got a winning formula. If you're tongue-tied, offer one of the following:

Seven Ways to Drink to Your Health

1. British: Cheers!
2. French: *À votre santé!*
3. German: *Prosit!*
4. Hebrew/Yiddish: *L'Chayim!*
5. Irish: *Sláinte!*
6. Italian: *Salute!*
7. Spanish: *Salud!*

May the road rise to meet you,
May the wind always be at your back,
May the sun shine warm upon your face,
the rains fall soft upon your fields,
And until we meet again,
May God hold you in the palm of his hand.

—Gaelic blessing

May you live all the years of your life.

—Jonathan Swift

Let us have wine and women
mirth and laughter,
Sermons and soda water the day after.

—Lord Byron

May you have the health of a salmon,
A strong heart, and a wet mouth.

—Unknown

DEALING WITH THE INEVITABLE—WHOOPS! AND OTHER PARTY MISHAPS

There will be times you'll wish your floor has a magic bottom—that if you make some blunder the floor will give way, swallowing you up and saving you from mortal embarrassment. Until that mystical moment arrives, relax. People don't expire, or even faint away, as a result of their faux pas. Handle your mishaps with grace and good humor and you'll put everyone else at ease.

I recall pouring hot mulled wine into a lovely pitcher. Unfortunately, I didn't test the pitcher first and realized too late that the glass couldn't withstand the heat. The pitcher literally split down its length and mulled cider trickled onto the table. All I could do was announce, "And now . . . for my next act . . ."

Broken Glasses

- If you're a guest, inform your host immediately if you break a glass. Clean up your mess as quickly as possible. If the glass isn't totally shattered, your host may want to get the piece repaired, especially if it's expensive or rare. Ask.
- Don't spend the evening playing the "blame game." If the glass broke while in your hands or your care, it's your problem. Tell your host you'll replace the item, then call later to get the details.
- On the other hand, as a host, you have to remember it's just glass. Don't whine. Don't glare at your accident-prone guest. But also, don't use your best crystal for a bash. Save it for subdued occasions.
- For safety's sake, if glass breaks near a bucket of ice, toss the ice.
- To avoid breakage, never add ice to a hot glass. The thermal shock could cause the glass to shatter. Don't clang two glasses together. When you toast, let the glasses gently kiss.

Is Your Wood Ruined? Maybe Not!

While cleaning up after the party, you may notice white rings made by wet glassware set directly on wooden tables. To remove these, try an oil and salt treatment. Mix ¼ cup vegetable oil with 1 teaspoon salt and gently massage into the wood. If that doesn't work, look for a commercial product in your hardware store.

Spilled Drinks

- "Who me? That spot wasn't there a minute ago." Sorry, but if you want to become a prized party animal you'll have to fess up to any spills. Besides, fabrics are less likely to become permanently stained if spills are treated immediately.
- Tell your host you spilled something and ask for cleaning materials.
- Offer to pay for any necessary dry cleaning.
- If you're the host and your carpet or tablecloth was damaged, see further on in this chapter for cleaning suggestions.

Where Do I Put My Glass?

Don't put a wet glass on a wood surface or you'll create water stains. If you don't have a coaster, ask your host what you should do with your glass. (As a good host, however, your guests shouldn't even have to ask. You'll have been prepared with oodles of clever coasters and handy cocktail napkins available at the bar.)

If you've had as much as you'd like of a drink, empty the glass to avoid accidents . . . but not in the plant please. There's nothing worse than a drunken rubber tree. Either

Holding a Glass Properly

- When filling a glass, hold it by the stem or base so you don't smudge the bowl of the glass with your fingerprints.
- As you sip, hold a white wine or champagne glass by the stem. You don't want to warm the wine with the heat of your hand.
- Hold a brandy glass by the base of the bowl so the warmth of your hand can release the spirit's aroma.

put the drink in the kitchen sink or ask the hostess what you should do.

When the party's over, wipe any telltale spots on wood surfaces with a dry cloth. Then go over the stain with furniture polish, using several coats if necessary to eliminate the stain. (See more tips throughout this chapter.)

Handling a Guest Who Drinks Too Much

It's easy to say, "Don't let this happen." But sometimes it does. You're pouring drinks, flitting among guests, passing food, and all the while an old buddy is slowly sinking under the coffee table.

As soon as you realize the problem, suggest that your guest come into the kitchen for a cup of bouillon or coffee. If your guest is very inebriated, he or she may be ready for a nap. It's not a bad idea to set up a cot in your den for such possibilities.

You have a moral, and possibly a legal, obligation to keep this guest from getting behind the wheel of a car. Don't ask your friends to drive a drunken guest home. That puts a burden on them in case the guest becomes surly or sick. In-

Tackling Stains

Quickly treating a spill means it's less likely to become a permanent stain.

Sprinkle fresh stains with salt to absorb the liquid. Then take a clean sponge, dip it in club soda, and dab at the spot. The carbonated bubbles may lift a new spot out. Blot thoroughly and allow to dry. To wash a stained tablecloth, first check the cleaning directions. See if there are any restrictions. If your fabric is durable, try the following: Mix a combination of 1 quart warm water; ½ teaspoon detergent; and 1 tablespoon plain, white vinegar. Soak the stained area in the mixture for 1 hour. Rinse well. If the stain persists, sponge with rubbing alcohol, rinse, and launder.

Other suggested treatments include:

- Rubbing a stain with lemon juice and salt. Let set 1 hour, then wash according to fabric directions.

- Holding the wine-stained area of the tablecloth over a heatproof bowl. Pour boiling water over the stain, letting it drip into the bowl.

stead, call a cab. As a last resort, make room in your home for an overnight visitor.

Taking Care of Yourself So You Don't Drink Too Much

Sometimes the tensions of getting ready for a party can lead to excessive drinking. You may find you're sampling the punch, trying out a new cocktail recipe, or having a drink to unwind before company comes. Before you know it, your brain is whirring.

You're less likely to overindulge if you avoid stress. Follow the tips in chapter 8 to give a foolproof party. Be sure you get plenty of sleep the night before. Get some exercise the afternoon of the big event and take a relaxing bath an hour before guests arrive.

If you do drink too much, take a break. Appoint a substitute host to mingle with your guests while you retreat to the kitchen for a cup of coffee or tea and a cheese or peanut butter sandwich. Eating food with a little fat can help your body absorb alcohol at a slower rate. If you've already drunk too much, a rich, high-fat cheese or similar food could make you feel queasy. You may prefer to skip food and wait it out. Time works wonders.

Enlist a friend to help you with the good-byes and leave cleaning up until morning.

THE PARTY'S OVER

Don't feel that you're being heartless just because you'd like to reclaim your living room. Your invitation stated the hours of the party, now it's time to move on. Unfortunately, some people may not be checking their watches or you may be giving mixed signals and people don't know if you're serious about ending the night. Ask a friend to make a show of leaving. That usually breaks up an event. If guests start milling, ask if you can help them find their coats. Thank people for coming. Otherwise, close the bar, clear the glassware and food, and turn off the music.

Cleaning Up

This is as much personal preference as it is a question of manners. Some hosts like having their friends help tidy up after a party. It's an opportunity for a postmortem. Others prefer to be left alone to deal with the mess.

If you're a host, don't ask for help, but accept it if you like. As a guest, don't feel obliged to volunteer unless you're a close friend.

The day after is a good time to take stock of the party. Don't beat yourself up over any mishaps but think about what you'd like to emphasize next time. Perhaps you'd like a co-host to make things run smoothly; maybe you invited too many people or not enough. Jot down the drinks everyone ordered or the food that disappeared instantly. You'll know what to serve next time. And just maybe you'll keep a list of favorite guests.

Food for the
Life of the Party

A Recipe Repertoire

The combination of spirits and conviviality whets appetites. You don't have to be a gourmet cook to follow the recipes for mouthwatering cocktail fare in this chapter. You'll shed your reputation as a cookaphobe when you serve Savory or Sweet Party Twists. Only you will know how easy the preparation is. And, if you'd like to offer something more exciting than a glass of wine with dinner, you'll be able to suggest some nifty food and cocktail pairings. Daiquiris with grilled red snapper, anyone?

There's nothing like sipping and chatting to build up an appetite. From the crunchy to the creamy, from the light and healthful to the rich—you'll find a plethora of fabulous and easy appetizer recipes in this chapter. Who would have thought that a six-inch plate could hold so much food?

Edibles are essential with drinks. There are the health arguments: People drink less when they eat and food settles their stomachs. And the culinary ones: Most alcoholic drinks taste better with food. Drinks taste less sour or less bitter when taken with a bite to eat. And don't forget the social pull of an attractive buffet table.

 ## PLANNING YOUR COCKTAIL PARTY MENU

Base the assortment and number of appetizers on the number of guests you have. For eight to twelve guests, three or four different hors d'oeuvres are sufficient. For thirteen to twenty-three guests, aim for five to six different appetizers. For larger parties of twenty-four to thirty guests, serve at least six to eight different appetizers.

For example, if you have eight guests you may want to prepare the following recipes. Assume everyone will want two to three servings of shrimp since it's so yummy, and then balance their plates with vegetables and an uptown take on guacamole and chips.

Shrimp Skewers with Mustard Sauce
Roasted Vegetables
Tomatillo Guacamole with Fresh Flour Tortilla Chips

Your menu for sixteen people could include:

Gorgonzola with Fig Jam
Salmon-Asparagus Packages
Steak with Mango Salsa
Savory Party Twists
Roasted Vegetables, but double the recipe

The amount people will eat depends on the type of food. If you're serving a substantial dish, such as Steak with Mango Salsa, figure about two ounces (or two strips of meat) per person. Guests will eat more of munchies, such as Curried, Candied Walnuts. And if you serve shrimp, put out double the amount you would of other foods. Everyone loves shrimp, say caterers.

Fun Fact!

The indentation you'll notice at the bottom of wine and champagne bottles is called a punt or a kick. The ingenious design traps the sediment at the bottom so it doesn't spread throughout the bottle. Contrary to what Cole Porter wrote, you do get a kick from champagne!

Let one food serve as the main attraction. Usually it's the protein food, such as shrimp or beef. Other foods are the supporting cast, but equally appealing. Choose recipes that offer a variety of flavors, colors, and textures. Crunch is good, but contrast it with creamy. Serve a platter of homemade tortilla chips with smooth guacamole, for example. Add color with bell pepper strips, broccoli florets, strawberries, grape clusters, and cherry tomatoes. Vary shapes—long skewers alternating with round, stuffed cabbages.

ADVANCE PREPARATION

Wouldn't you rather rub shoulders than chop celery when your friends arrive? No one will know how easy it was for you to prepare such a tempting array of dishes. Here are some ways you can get a jump on party cooking:

Bake breads, and cookies several weeks in advance and freeze. Wrap packages in a layer of plastic wrap and a second layer of aluminum foil to keep air out. Baked goods will retain their quality if thawed in the refrigerator. However, if you don't have refrigerator space, plain breads and similar foods won't spoil if left on the counter to thaw. Freshen the texture by baking these foods for five minutes at 350 degrees F.

Soft cheese spreads can also be frozen. These must be thawed in the refrigerator. Allow up to two days to defrost.

Do not freeze raw vegetables. They'll develop an unpleasant texture.

Do not refrigerate tomatoes. They become starchy tasting.

If you're stocking up on fresh mint or other herbs for garnishes, wrap the stems in a damp paper towel. Then wrap the towel in plastic wrap to retain the moisture. Refrigerate up to four days, changing the wrappings as necessary to keep moist.

Put plates, silverware, and napkins on the table a day in advance.

Get the food on the table just before guests arrive.

> **Helpful Hint**
>
> Enlist a friend to keep an eye on the hors d'oeuvres. Remove platters when they're half empty, refill in the kitchen, and return to the table.

CAN-OPENER CHALLENGED?

"I can't cook, don't ask me." You, too, can put out a stylish spread, the envy of what's-her-name, even if you don't own a stove. Here are some delicious ideas:

1. Buy an assortment of good-quality European olives such as niçoise or kalamata. Put them in individual, small ceramic bowls.

2. Buy precooked jumbo shrimp. Arrange on a bed of arugula or mixed baby greens. Mix

> **Helpful Hint**
>
> You'll discover the reason why parsley was invented as you plate food. Stuffed cherry tomatoes or skewered shrimp slip and slide and look naked on the plate. But if you first line your platter with bunches of parsley, then add your shrimp, it will be anchored on a beautiful field of greens.

together equal parts mayonnaise and salsa. Set in a scooped-out orange shell and use as a dip.

3. Arrange precooked chicken wings on a tray. Mix together equal parts mayonnaise and mango chutney. Spoon into a bowl and serve as a dip.

4. Thoroughly drain a can of garbanzo beans and dry them on paper towels. Sprinkle generously with fresh ground black pepper. Serve as a snack. (You may not believe this but garbanzo beans are a delicious morsel.)

5. Hollow out a round French bread. Feed the crumbs to the birds and fill the shell with deli crabmeat salad; surround with crackers or celery stalks.

6. Buy a container of processed cheese spread. Bring to room temperature to soften. Spread between minicrackers to make your own cheese sandwiches. Get fancy and roll the cheese filling in finely chopped pecans if you like.

7. Take the pimiento out of stuffed green olives and substitute cooked, frozen, or canned baby shrimp.

8. Bake preformed filo dough cups according to package directions. Fill each with a spoonful of either goat cheese, ricotta cheese, or olive paste.

9. Spread a flour tortilla with softened salmon-flavored cream cheese. Roll up tightly into a tube. Slice ½-inch thick crosswise into pinwheels.

10. Wrap slices of deli turkey breast meat around avocado wedges. Secure with toothpicks. Mix together equal parts mayonnaise and mustard and add a dash of

curry powder. Spoon into a bowl and add a spoon. Let guests spread on sauce.

FABULOUS, FESTIVE, AND FAST RECIPES

CURRIED, CANDIED WALNUTS

Spiced nuts are an addictive addition to a cocktail party menu. This hot and sweet version has a crisp sugar shell.

1   **cup sugar**

¼   **teaspoon salt**

½   **teaspoon hot curry powder**

¼   **teaspoon cayenne pepper**

Grated rind of 2 oranges

2 cups walnut halves

Butter

In a small, heavy-bottomed pot, combine sugar, salt, curry powder, cayenne pepper, and orange rind. Stir well. Cook mixture over medium heat, stirring occasionally with wooden spoon, until sugar melts and turns golden, about 15 to 20 minutes. Do not allow the mixture to boil or it may burn. Quickly stir in walnut halves to coat.

> **Fun Fact!**
>
> You've heard of a bumper crop of potatoes or corn. To a farmer the term "bumper" means an abundant harvest. But to a drinker, "bumper" is an old English term for a cup filled to the brim.

Spread mixture out on well-buttered cookie sheet. Set aside for candy coating to cool and harden. Using buttered hands or a buttered knife, break nut mixture into bite-size pieces.

Makes 2¼ cups (20 servings).

Party tip: These nuts get soggy if left at room temperature. Make a day in advance and store in a plastic container with a tight-fitting lid.

GORGONZOLA WITH FIG JAM

Gorgonzola dolce is an Italian blue cheese that's milder and sweeter than the better-known Gorgonzola. You'll find it in many gourmet food stores and in cheese shops.

1   (8-ounce) wedge Gorgonzola dolce

1   baguette bread, sliced into 16 pieces

1   cup fig jam

16 walnut halves

This do-it-yourself appetizer is greater than its parts. Put out a wedge of cheese and surround it with the sliced bread. Spoon the jam into an attractive dish (add a small serving spoon) and put the nuts in a bowl.

Allow guests to put a hunk of cheese on bread, top it with a tablespoon of jam, and finish with a walnut half.

Makes 16 servings.

Party tip: Set cheese out an hour before the party so it comes to room temperature. It will be more flavorful and easier to spread. If you prefer, substitute a combination of blue cheese and apricot jam, Brie and raspberry jam, or goat cheese and tomato jam.

ENDIVE BITES

Fill juicy and slightly bitter Belgian endive leaves with a savory cheddar cheese spread. The combination is as delicious as it is attractive. Roasted red pepper strips can be purchased (usually packed in jars) at your local supermarket.

1   carton (8-ounces) sharp cheddar cheese food

¼   teaspoon hot paprika

⅛   teaspoon ground cumin

⅛   teaspoon hot chile powder

1   tablespoon minced chives

2   tablespoons half-and-half

4   heads Belgian endive (you should have at least 32 large leaves)

32 small roasted red pepper strips

In a blender, combine cheese food, paprika, cumin, chile powder, chives, and half-and-half.

Separate endive heads into individual leaves. Wash each leaf and pat dry. Spoon ½ tablespoon of the cheese spread on the tip of each leaf. Garnish cheese spread with a piece of red pepper.

Makes 32 appetizer servings.

Party tip: The cheese spread may be prepared up to two days in advance and refrigerated. Assemble the leaves up to 4 hours ahead, cover with plastic wrap, and refrigerate.

PIZZA PUFFS

Cookbook author Marilyn Tausend shares her tip for almost-instant pizzas. She bakes flour tortillas in a hot oven just until they balloon into crisp puffs. Then she adds toppings, heats the pizza puffs, and lets people tear off bites. Here are two variations of her idea.

Provencal Puffs

3   (8-inch) flour tortillas

1½ cups grated mozzarella

1½ cups finely diced plum tomatoes

6   tablespoons minced, pitted niçoise olives

3   teaspoons minced fresh basil

3   teaspoons extra-virgin olive oil

Salt and freshly ground pepper to taste

Preheat oven to 400 degrees F.

Place tortillas on oven racks. Heat for 2 to 3 minutes, or until tortillas puff up. Remove from oven. Place tortillas on cookie sheet. Sprinkle each tortilla with ½ cup of the mozzarella, ½ cup of the tomatoes, 2 tablespoons of the olives, and 1 teaspoon of the basil. Then drizzle each with 1 teaspoon olive oil and sprinkle with salt and pepper. Return to oven for 2 to 3 minutes, or until cheese melts.

To serve, place tortillas on serving platters. Let guests tear off pieces.

Makes 12 appetizer servings.

Mediterranean Puffs

1½ tablespoons extra-virgin olive oil

2   packed cups coarsely sliced radicchio

½   teaspoon white balsamic vinegar

¼   teaspoon salt

⅛   teaspoon pepper

2   (8-inch) flour tortillas

4   fresh black or green figs, cut horizontally into ½-inch thick slices

½   cup grated Parmesan cheese

¼   cup chopped walnuts

Preheat oven to 400 degrees F.

In medium skillet, heat oil. Add radicchio. Sauté 5 minutes or until tender. Stir in vinegar, salt, and pepper and sauté 30 seconds. Set aside.

Place tortillas on oven racks. Heat for 2 to 3 minutes, or until tortillas puff up. Remove from oven.

Spread radicchio over crusts. Arrange fig slices over radicchio. Sprinkle half the cheese and walnuts over each tortilla. Return to oven and bake 3 minutes, or until cheese is soft.

To serve, place tortillas on serving platters. Let guests tear off pieces.

Makes 8 appetizer servings.

Party tip: Make puffs up to an hour in advance and serve at room temperature if desired.

ROASTED VEGETABLES

Instead of putting out the standard raw platter, roast a combination of vegetables such as the mushrooms and asparagus combination below. Other good vegetables to try are bell peppers, brussels sprouts, and onions. The high oven temperature brings out the vegetables' natural sugars and an Asian-influenced dipping sauce rounds out the flavors.

6   portobello mushrooms, stems removed

1   pound fat asparagus, tough ends snapped off

½   teaspoon each salt and pepper

2   tablespoons olive oil

2   teaspoons white wine vinegar

¼   cup soy sauce

2   tablespoons balsamic vinegar

½   teaspoon grated gingerroot

1   tablespoon brown sugar

Preheat oven to 400 degrees F.

Brush any dirt from mushrooms. Cut into quarters and place in large roasting pan. Cut asparagus into 2-inch lengths and add to pan. Sprinkle with salt, pepper, olive oil, and white wine vinegar. Roast for 15 to 20 minutes or until asparagus are tender. Remove from oven.

In a bowl, combine soy sauce, balsamic vinegar, gingerroot, and brown sugar. Stir well.

Place vegetables on a serving platter and arrange dipping sauce in the center. Set out forks for service.

Makes 8 appetizer servings.

Party tips: Make the dipping sauce in advance. Roast the vegetables up to 2 hours in advance and keep at room temperature.

SALMON-ASPARAGUS PACKAGES

Smoked salmon is so elegant, yet so easy to work with. It's a beautiful wrapper for chunks of cooked asparagus. Seal your bundles with chives and dress them with a zesty jalapeño-chile vinaigrette.

2 tablespoons lime juice

¼ teaspoon salt

¼ cup extra-virgin olive oil

¼ teaspoon freshly ground black pepper

1 small jalapeño chile, cored, seeded, and minced

8 short, fat asparagus

16 slices smoked salmon

16 long whole chives

In a cup, stir together lime juice and salt until salt dissolves. Add olive oil and pepper. Stir in chile. Set aside.

Snap off tough ends of asparagus. Arrange asparagus in small skillet with water to cover. Bring to a boil. Reduce heat to medium and cook until asparagus are fork tender, but still a vivid green color, about 10 minutes. Remove from heat. Drain. Run asparagus under cold water to chill. Cut each asparagus in half widthwise.

Wrap one slice salmon around each asparagus piece. Wrap one chive around each bundle and gently tie with a bow in the front. Arrange asparagus bundles on a serving platter. Spoon chile vinaigrette over asparagus. Either serve with forks, or add toothpicks for spearing a serving.

Makes 16 servings.

Party tip: The bundles and the vinaigrette can be made a day in advance. Wrap separately and refrigerate. Bring the dressing to room temperature and pour over asparagus just before serving.

SHRIMP SKEWERS WITH MUSTARD SAUCE

You can cook the shrimp and mix the mustard sauce a day in advance. Keep both in tightly sealed containers in the refrigerator. In addition to the ingredients listed below, you'll also need a supply of wooden skewers.

Shrimp Skewers

1   lemon, thinly sliced

20 peppercorns

1   garlic clove, peeled and smashed

1   teaspoon salt

24 raw jumbo shrimp, unpeeled

48 cherry tomatoes

Mustard sauce (follows)

In a large pot, combine 2 quarts water, lemon slices, peppercorns, garlic, and salt. Add shrimp. Bring to a boil. Turn off heat. Let shrimp sit in mixture 5 minutes. Drain, cool, and peel.

To serve, skewer one cherry tomato on a wooden skewer. Add a shrimp and top with a second tomato. Repeat to fill 24 skewers.

Prepare mustard sauce.

Arrange shrimp on a platter and spoon sauce into a bowl.

Makes 24 appetizer servings.

Mustard Sauce

- ½ **cup sour cream**
- ½ **cup mayonnaise**
- 2 **tablespoons Dijon-style mustard**
- 2 **tablespoons minced Italian parsley**
- 1 **teaspoon fresh lemon juice**
- ¼ **teaspoon pepper**

In a bowl, stir together sour cream, mayonnaise, mustard, parsley, lemon juice, and pepper.

Makes about 1¼ cups.

STEAK WITH MANGO SALSA

To update the classic steak and Martini duo, couple the beef with a refreshing Mango Salsa. Five-spice powder gives the meat a rich and complex flavor.

Steak

- 2 **(1-pound) strip steaks, cut 1-inch thick**
- 1 **teaspoon five-spice powder**
- ½ **teaspoon each salt and pepper**
- ¼ **cup balsamic vinegar**
- **Mango Salsa (recipe follows)**
- 1 **baguette, cut into 16 slices**

Place steaks in shallow bowl. Rub each side with ¼-teaspoon five-spice powder. Season steaks with salt and pepper. Pour vinegar over steaks. Set steaks aside to marinate at room temperature for 30 minutes, occasionally turning to coat with vinegar.

Preheat broiler. Meanwhile, prepare Mango Salsa.
Place steaks on oil-coated broiler rack over a pan.
Place under preheated grill, set 4 inches from heat.
Grill steaks 5 to 6 minutes per side for medium-rare.
Remove from grill immediately and set aside for 5
minutes.

Using a sharp knife, slice steaks ¼-inch thick, for a
total of 32 slices. Arrange in a fan shape on a large
serving platter. Set Mango Salsa in a bowl in the center
of the platter. Arrange sliced bread in a basket.

To serve, guests may arrange 2 steak slices on a
piece of bread and top with a dollop of salsa. Steak and
salsa may also be served without bread.

Makes about 16 appetizer servings.

Mango Salsa

2	medium mangoes
½	cup finely chopped red onion
1	jalapeño chile, cored, seeded, and minced
1	tablespoon fresh lime juice
2	tablespoons minced cilantro
⅛	teaspoon hot chile powder
¼	teaspoon each salt and pepper

Peel mangoes and slice into chunks. Cut chunks into
½-inch dices. There should be about 2 cups. Place in a
bowl. Add onion, chile, lime juice, cilantro, chile powder, salt. and pepper. Set aside for 10 minutes for flavors to blend.

Makes about 2½ cups.

*Party tips: The Steak and Mango Salsa may also be
served in flour tortillas for a buffet dinner. The salsa may*

be prepared a day in advance and refrigerated. Lean pork tenderloin may be used in place of the steak. Cook the pork until a meat thermometer registers 160 degrees. You may also cook the meat ahead of time and serve this dish at room temperature if you prefer.

STUFFED TOMATOES

If you can find baby balls of fresh mozzarella use them for this appetizer. The tender, buttery cheese is just the right size to pack into a large cherry tomato.

20 cherry tomatoes

20 cubes mozzarella cheese, in ½-inch dices

20 strips sun-dried tomato (oil-packed)

20 small basil leaves

Basil sprigs for garnish

Cut off top third of each cherry tomato. Using a small, serrated spoon, scoop out the seeds and pulp. Add a cheese cube, sun-dried tomato strip, and basil leaf. Arrange on platter. Decorate with basil sprigs.

Makes 20 servings.

Party tip: Cherry tomatoes can be stuffed with a variety of fillings. Try an olive paste, guacamole, flavored cream cheese, or baby shrimp. You can make this appetizer up to one hour in advance, but do not refrigerate the tomatoes. It kills the flavor.

TUSCAN BEAN BRUSCHETTA

You've done hummus and pita bread. Now it's time for its classy Italian cousin, Tuscan Bean Bruschetta. This open-faced mini sandwich of beans, garlic, and Parmesan cheese is substantial enough to make a light dinner entree. The roasted garlic paste can be obtained at many finer supermarkets.

1   can (15-ounces) cannellini beans, drained and rinsed

1   tablespoon roasted garlic paste

⅓   cup grated Parmesan cheese

1   teaspoon minced fresh rosemary or ½ teaspoon crushed, dried rosemary

¼   teaspoon freshly grated pepper

1   teaspoon grated lemon rind

16 slices cocktail rye bread

Preheat oven to 375 degrees F.

In a blender, combine beans, garlic paste, cheese, rosemary, pepper, and lemon rind. Puree. Spread 1 heaping tablespoon of bean puree on each bread slice.

Arrange on cookie sheet. Bake for 5 minutes or until bread is toasted and hot.

Makes 16 appetizers.

Party tips: The bean mixture may be made a day in advance and refrigerated. Spread the bread up to 4 hours in advance, cover, and refrigerate, toasting just before serving. The bean puree, packed in a hollowed-out red bell pepper shell, also makes an excellent dip for spicy tortilla chips.

Light Hors d'Oeuvres

CHEDDAR BITS

Cookies and crackers the size of a nickel are all the rage in gourmet food stores. But you can easily make these mini-morsels to have on hand for parties. Cheddar Bits and Martinis are a great combination.

¼ cup unsalted butter

4 ounces (1 packed cup) grated sharp cheddar cheese

1 teaspoon hot red pepper sauce

½ teaspoon salt

⅔ cup flour

Preheat oven to 375 degrees F.

In the bowl of a heavy-duty mixer, cream the butter. Gradually beat in cheese by the tablespoon. Blend in red pepper sauce and salt. Blend in flour. Dough will be crumbly. Scoop out dough by the rounded tablespoon. Roll into marble-sized balls.

Place on ungreased cookie sheet, 1 inch apart. Bake until lightly browned, about 13 to 15 minutes.

Makes 36.

Party tip: Cheddar Bits may be prepared up to two months in advance and frozen. Store bits in an airtight freezer bag. To serve, thaw in refrigerator overnight. If you want to serve these warm, arrange on a cookie sheet and warm in an oven preheated to 350 degrees for about 5 minutes.

SAVORY PARTY TWISTS

Start with puff pastry and add some bite to your nibbles. You'll find chipotle chile powder in the spice section of better supermarkets.

1   sheet frozen puff pastry, thawed (see note)

2   egg whites

1   cup grated Parmesan cheese

¼   teaspoon chipotle chili powder or spicy paprika

¼   teaspoon garlic salt

Preheat oven to 375 degrees F.

Unfold puff pastry and cut into 3 (10-inch long, 3-inch wide) strips. Cut each strip into 10 smaller strips: 3 inches long, 1 inch wide.

Beat egg whites in a bowl. On a plate stir together cheese, chili powder, and garlic salt.

Dip each puff pastry strip into the egg white, then into the cheese mixture to lightly coat. Make one twist in each strip and place 1 inch apart on well-greased cookie sheet. Bake until golden, about 10 minutes. Remove to wire racks and cool.

Makes 30 twists.

Note: Frozen puff pastry is available in the frozen dessert section of supermarkets. The product comes two sheets to a package. The remaining sheet may be used for Sweet Party Twists.

Party tip: Puff pastry is best baked just before serving, but twists can be made in advance and frozen. Slightly underbake by a minute or two. Cool twists and freeze in plastic containers up to a month. Thaw twists in refrigerator overnight. Arrange on cookie sheet and toast in an over preheated to 350 degrees 2 to 3 minutes. Serve immediately.

SWEET PARTY TWISTS

These light, crisp mouthfuls take minutes to make, and even less time to devour. Pair these with frothy Ginger Champagne or White Wine Spritzers.

1   sheet frozen puff pastry, thawed (see note below)

2   egg whites

3   tablespoons sugar

1   cup finely chopped walnuts

¼   teaspoon cinnamon

¼   teaspoon salt

Preheat oven to 400 degrees F.

Unfold puff pastry sheet and cut into 3 (10-inch long, 3-inch wide) strips. Cut each strip into 10 smaller strips: 3 inches long, 1 inch wide.

Beat egg whites with 1 tablespoon of the sugar in a bowl. On a plate, stir together the remaining 2 tablespoons sugar, nuts, cinnamon, and salt.

Dip each puff pastry strip into the egg white mixture, then into the sugared nuts to lightly coat. Make one twist in each strip and place 1 inch apart on a greased cookie sheet. Bake until golden, 10 to 13 minutes. Remove to wire racks and cool.

Makes 30 twists.

Note: Frozen puff pastry is available in the frozen dessert section of supermarkets. The product comes two sheets to a package. The other sheet may be used for Savory Party Twists, or simply double the recipe—people love these.

TOMATILLO GUACAMOLE
WITH FRESH FLOUR TORTILLA CHIPS

Tomatillos resemble green husk-covered tomatoes. They have a wonderful citrus-like taste. They're fleshy, not juicy, producing a dryer, creamier guacamole. If you can't find tomatillos, use red tomatoes instead.

Tomatillo Guacamole

Fresh flour tortilla chips (recipe follows)

1   **large shallot, peeled and quartered**

2   **small tomatillos, flaky outside skin removed, cored, and quartered**

2   **small avocados, peeled and pitted**

1   **jalapeño chile, cored, seeded, and quartered**

¼   **teaspoon ground cumin**

½   **teaspoon salt**

1   **tablespoon minced fresh cilantro**

Prepare tortilla chips according to the recipe below. Set aside when done.

Prepare guacamole. In the bowl of a food processor fitted with a steel blade, combine shallot, tomatillos, avocados, and jalapeño. Process with on/off turns until mixture is minced, about 15 turns. Remove to a bowl. Stir in cumin, salt, and cilantro.

To serve, arrange chips on a platter. Place bowl with guacamole in the center.

Makes 2 cups guacamole.

Fresh Flour Tortilla Chips

4   (8-inch) flour tortillas

Olive-oil flavored cooking spray

½   teaspoon coarse sea salt or regular salt

Preheat oven to 400 degrees F.

Place tortillas on cookie sheet. Spray with cooking spray. Sprinkle each tortilla with ⅛ teaspoon salt. Cut each tortilla into 6 wedges. Bake until firm and lightly browned, 2 to 3 minutes. Immediately remove from oven and from cooking sheet to keep from further cooking.

Makes 24 chips.

Party tips: Bake the chips a day in advance and store in an airtight container or use the best-quality thick store-bought tortilla chips you can find. If possible, make the guacamole just before serving. This guacamole recipe is more durable than many and is slower to turn brown. You can make it up to 2 hours in advance.

TOMATO HUMMUS AND PITA WEDGES

Your health-conscious guests will appreciate having a dip that delivers full flavor with a fraction of the fat of most dip recipes. Each serving has only 3 grams of fat.

½ cup finely chopped onion

1 garlic clove, minced

2 tablespoons chicken or vegetable broth

3 large plum tomatoes, cored and finely chopped

1 cup lowfat hummus

1 tablespoon minced fresh mint, plus sprigs for garnish

4 whole wheat pita breads, cut into wedges

In a small skillet, combine onion, garlic, and chicken broth. Sauté over low heat 5 minutes, until onion is tender. Add tomatoes and cook over medium heat until mixture is thick, pulpy, and almost dry, about 10 minutes.

Spoon into a bowl and cool to room temperature. Stir in hummus and minced mint. Garnish with mint sprigs. Serve as dip with pita bread.

Makes 2 cups.

Party tips: Use a commercially prepared, plain hummus. Stir in the tomato mixture up to one day in advance and store in the refrigerator.

COCKTAILS AND DINNER

"Well, um, I'll have a glass of wine." You probably hear that all the time when you ask your dinner guests what they'd like to drink. You say it yourself when you go to someone else's home. It's not that you're really interested in wine. If you were you'd probably say, "Give me a Merlot and make it a '96 from Joe's vineyard" to show you know your grapes. People usually ask for wine because they don't know what else to ask for, or don't know what you've got to offer.

But you've learned about drinks in *The Absolute Beginner's Guide,* and there's no reason you should pour a glass of white wine when you could be blending a Daiquiri. Make a show of it. After all, a

> ## Helpful Hint
> Cocktails and dessert anyone? Add a kick to your homemade chocolate fudge and truffles by adding a quarter cup of scotch or brandy to a recipe. Serve these sweets along with coffee after dinner.

dinner party is an evening's entertainment. Select one, two, or three cocktails that are appropriate to your menu. You can create a theme by flavor, ethnic influence, or ingredients. Make drink cards describing your cocktail repertoire for the evening.

For example, if you're serving a spicy southwestern chili, start with a hot Bloody Mary with a habanero chile garnish. That should heat up your party. Then switch to Sangria with the meal. To accompany paella, the Spanish seafood and poultry rice dish, serve a sophisticated Finotini. Perhaps you're celebrating the delicious fall apple crop. Let your guests sip Sour Apple Martinis as they await a sumptuous pork and apple stew.

Place all the ingredients for your dinner cocktails on a side table or rolling cart and perform your mixology magic to an appreciative audience. When you're ready to serve dinner, remove the cart and clear the drink glasses. Serve whatever wines or other beverages you have planned.

Some menus and cocktails fit together like an olive and a Martini. Here are some combinations you may want to serve:

Martini with steak or broiled lobster
Bloody Mary with chili
Black Velvet with prime rib
Daiquiri with grilled red snapper or grouper
Cuba Libre with arroz con pollo or Caribbean rice and
    bean dishes
Cosmopolitan with anything new and American
Saketini with sushi

Your guests will appreciate any effort you make to keep them well-fed. No one—at least no one you'd want to invite to your home—will complain that the mustard didn't come from Dijon, France, or that the bread wasn't hearth-baked. So don't worry that your cooking isn't complicated or showy or that you can't afford caviar. None of that is necessary. You have plenty of easy and delicious food choices your friends will love.

Frequently Asked Questions

On your way to becoming a great mixologist and party host or hostess, you may encounter situations that aren't covered in the standard drink books: what to do with the inch of gin that's left in a bottle or how to follow a low-carbohydrate diet and still drink alcohol. *The Absolute Beginner's Guide to Mixing Drinks* takes these issues into account. Here you'll find answers to both serious and tongue-in-cheek questions.

There's no question too basic for the *Absolute Beginner's Guide.* How will you learn unless you ask? If you didn't find the information you needed in the previous chapters, perhaps the answers to these common queries will help you as well.

Q. Can I make my own spirits?

A. Some states will allow you to make wine or beer strictly for your own use. Check with your state regulators to see what the license requirements are.

Q. I'd like to use alcohol in a recipe I'm serving to children. Does cooking destroy alcohol?

A. According to several university experiments, cooking causes almost all, but not all, alcohol to evaporate. The longer you cook the dish, the less alcohol you'll have in the final product. For example, food cooked for 30 minutes loses about 95 percent of its alcohol. If you're serving someone who must abstain from alcohol, do not assume that a cooked dish is safe. Instead, buy a nonalcoholic wine or substitute fruit juice or bouillon in your recipe. If you do cook with alcohol, keep the lid off the food for at least 30 minutes. A lid will trap the alcohol, cause it to condense and drip back into your dish.

Q. How should I store alcohol once I've opened a bottle?

A. Keep it tightly capped in its original bottle away from light and heat. Use decanters only for spirits that you'll drink within a few weeks. Wine-based alcohol such as sherry, port, and vermouth loses its freshness sooner than grain-based liquors. Store sherry, port, and vermouth in the refrigerator and use within a few weeks. Brandy, with its higher alcohol content, should keep for years.

Q. I just discovered several bottles of spirits I had stored in the garage for years. Are they still okay to drink?

A. Never-opened bottles that were kept out of direct light and not subjected to extremes of heat and cold should be fine. Bottles that have been opened but are tightly closed will also be potable as long as the bottle is still at least ¼ full. If you only have an inch or so left in the bottle, it's likely the flavor evaporated into the bottle's airspace. Discard the product.

Q. Can I use light and dark rum interchangeably in a cocktail?

A. Although light and dark rum start with the same base, fermented sugarcane, the manufacturing process results in the differing shades and flavors. This author recommends you do not substitute, but use the rum specified in the recipes.

However, you may want to experiment. Light rum, which is also referred to as clear or silver, is aged in uncharred oak barrels. Its flavor is so subtle you can substitute it for vodka in many drinks. If you don't believe it, try a Rumtini. Golden rum, the color of whiskey, is mellower in flavor. You could use it in place of light rum in a Piña Colada; the drink will be more robust tasting. Dark rum, the color of molasses, has a very robust taste. A dark rum, such as Myers, will not be tasty in a Martini but it is great in punches and fruity drinks. Dark rum will also turn your aunt's fruitcake into a delicious mouthful. See the next question.

Q. Why do cooks add rum or other liquors to cakes? What do they do?

A. A robust liquor adds flavor and moisture to a cake. Start with a recipe for a dense, fruity cake. (A chiffon cake will become a sodden mess.) Let the cake cool for a day or two, then brush with a couple of tablespoons of dark rum or bourbon. Wrap the cake in a double layer of aluminum foil and set aside in a cool, dark place. Repeat this process two or three times a week for up to two weeks, and use within a month of soaking.

Q. Speaking of cooking, how do you use spirits in recipes?

A. The general rule is to never cook with a liquor you wouldn't want to drink. Heat evaporates most of the alcohol, but leaves the flavor. For soups and stews, add spirits at the point when the dish should be simmered. Long, slow cooking will get rid of the raw taste. For desserts, add the liquor along with or instead of an extract. Liquor is a bold flavoring. Don't go overboard. Use a little to add a subtle touch.

Q. What do the letters V.S.O.P. mean on a bottle of Cognac?

A. These are indications of a Cognac's quality. V.S.O.P. stands for "Very Superior Old Pale." It's not the finest you can buy, but it's P.D.G. (pretty darn good). X.O., which means "Extra Old," is considered the finest quality available to most consumers.

Q. What is a fortified wine and how do I serve it?

A. A wine that's blended with a distilled spirit, usually brandy, is "fortified." Sherry, Madeira, and port are examples of fortified wines. Serve a dry fortified wine as an aperitif or cocktail-hour drink. Serve a sweet wine after dinner instead of dessert. Although fortified wines are rarely used in mixed drinks, a splash of port does wonders for Sangria.

Q. A case of champagne made a bumpy ride to our home. Should I take any precautions when opening one of these bottles?

A. Wait at least a day before opening a champagne bottle that's been shaken up. Then when you do open it, follow the directions given earlier in chapter 9, "Opening Champagne with Finesse."

Q. We received a beautiful crystal decanter for a present. Is this safe for storing spirits?

A. Traditionally crystal is made by combining quartz with lead compounds. Some health experts suggest that when lead crystal comes into contact with acidic beverages some of the lead leaches into the liquid. The amount of lead that might dissolve in your liquor depends on the lead content of your decanter, the product you're storing, and how long the product stays in the decanter. Citrus-enhanced liquors may be a problem. Wine, port, and sherry may dissolve more lead than scotch and vodka. You're likely to be safe for lead levels if you pour just enough nonacidic liquor into a decanter to use for one party. Don't use your decanter to display liquor.

Q. Help. I have a food intolerance to wheat products. Are there any spirits I can drink?

A. You should see an allergy specialist before drinking anything that could make you physically ill. That said, your best bets are Cognac, brandy, rum, good-quality tequila, and vodka made from potatoes, not grain.

Q. Do I have to use a green olive in a Martini?

A. No. A green olive has a distinctive nutty flavor and a balance of acid and salt that enhances a Martini, but you can certainly experiment. Try a pickled jalapeño, a fruity-tasting, black niçoise olive, or a strip of roasted red bell pepper.

Q. I have fifty people coming for a cocktail party. Can I mix drinks in advance?

A. It would certainly be a great convenience, but many drinks taste flat if made too far ahead of time. Fruit-based drinks develop a little bitterness and vodka loses its tingle. Make drinks to order or at most an hour in advance and keep chilled. Another option is to prepare two or three pitcher drinks. The base for Sangria and other fruit punches can be made several hours in advance. Stir and add club soda or other mixers just before serving.

Q. I'm on a low-carbohydrate weight-loss diet. Can I drink alcoholic beverages?

A. If you're trying to reduce carbs, choose hard liquor, such as gin, vodka, or whiskey, which have low or almost no carbohydrates. Dry wines are also a good choice. Sweet wines, such as French Sauternes, have about 7 grams of carbohydrates in a 7-ounce serving.

The carbohydrates in beer range from 4 to 11 grams per 12-ounce serving. You'll want to skip the classic cocktails and liqueurs. Gin and Tonic weighs in with almost 16 grams of carbohydrates and crème de menthe at 21 grams of carbohydrates for a 1½-ounce serving. Remember that calories still count. See chapter 7 for tips on drinking and dieting.

Q. Some people insist on vodka for Martinis; other people only want gin. Are these interchangeable, or is one better than the other?

A. It's really a matter of preference. The Martini is an evolving drink. The original Martini was sweet. Now the preference is for a dry Martini made with vodka, which is odorless and tasteless (except for seasoned vodkas). When you use vodka in a Martini, you get a clean tasting drink. Gin, with its complex recipe of juniper berries and herbs (which might include coriander, angelica, cardamom, cinnamon, licorice, and caraway), adds flavor and character to a Martini. You probably note a bias here, but the choice is yours.

Q. Some classic drinks such as a Ramos gin fizz or a pink lady use raw egg whites. I've read that raw egg whites might lead to food-borne illness. Are these drinks safe?

A. Raw egg whites were whipped into these gin-based drinks to make them frothier. However, that practice is risky now. A small percentage of eggs carry salmonella bacteria. Cooking is the only way to destroy salmonella, which can cause severe stomach upset. For most people the misery passes in a day or two, but people with compromised immune systems, such as the elderly or those who have cancer, could suffer severe consequences from salmonella poisoning. Either use pasteurized raw egg whites available in some supermarkets or eliminate the whites altogether. You won't notice a difference in taste.

Q. What about that worm in tequila? Is that real or an urban legend?

A. There's no worm in tequila. Mescal contains a caterpillar, not a worm, though the distinction may be lost on you if you're "fortunate" enough to swallow it. Getting the caterpillar is supposed to bring good luck.

Q. I'm confused about all those "cactus" liquors. Can you explain what cactus-based spirits are?

A. Several popular Mexican liquors are processed from various species of the agave plant, which is not a cactus, though it resembles one. This succulent plant, also called maguey, has fat, spear-like leaves and a tall-stemmed flower. The differing plant species are turned into tequila, mescal, or pulque.

Pulque is a mildly intoxicating, milky white beverage. You can mix it with fruit juices, spices, sugar, or cream, but it's not a bar drink that you'll see much of in the United States.

Mescal is a clear and potent spirit with a characteristic smoky taste. It's produced from agave that grows in Mexico's warmer regions. Mescal may be refined and smooth; or it can be raw and fiery.

Tequila is regulated by Mexican law, which sets quality standards. The pure distilled product is clear and colorless but can be aged in oak for flavor and color. By law tequila must be made from the blue variety of agave, which has a distinctive flavor. Tequila is so trendy now, you'll find better bars offering a wide sampling of the liquor.

Q. What's the difference between a cordial and a liqueur?

A. Only the words. Both cordials and liqueurs have the same basic recipe: sweetened spirits flavored with fruits, herbs, barks, and other seasoning ingredients. A fruit-flavored brandy is less sweet and more potent than a liqueur. An eau-de-vie, another member of the fruit-based spirits family, is distilled from fermented fruit juice. Kirsch, with its delicate cherry scent, is an eau-de-vie.

Q. Drinking warms me up on a cold night, but I've read that people shouldn't drink alcoholic beverages when out in the cold. Why not?

A. Although you may feel "warm" when you drink, it's an illusion. Alcohol causes blood to flow through your body more readily. The flush you may experience while drinking is an example of this. Alcohol actually lowers your body temperature. If you're trapped in a snowstorm the last thing you want to do is reduce your body temperature.

Q. I've read about absinthe, which seems like an exotic liquor. What is it and where can I find it?

A. Absinthe is the stuff of literature, not bar drinks. It's illegal in the United States. The liquor, a blend of herbs, including wormwood, is extremely potent and potentially damaging to the human nervous system. You can enjoy the anise flavor of absinthe in other liquors, such as anisette.

Q. When I buy rubbing alcohol in a drug store, am I getting a spirit I can drink?

A. No. Only ethyl alcohol is safe to drink. Isopropyl alcohol, or rubbing alcohol, and methyl, or wood alcohol, are dangerously toxic.

Q. Won't vodka freeze if I put it in the freezer for a few hours?

A. No. Because of its high alcohol level, vodka won't freeze. It will become very cold. Some Martini lovers don't recommend this. They prefer room-temperature gin or vodka, which melts a little of the ice during preparation and dilutes the drink. You'll note that alcohol's antifreeze properties are also at work if you make an ice cream with a high proportion of alcohol. You'll get slush, not a frozen dessert.

Q. Can you bruise gin if you shake it?
A. No. Liquids don't "bruise."

Glossary of
Popular Drink Terms

Your drink can be muddled—mixed with mashed herbs or flavorings—but *you* shouldn't be. Master the bartender's vocabulary and you'll know the difference between shaking and blending. You'll be privy to a secret language—a pony's worth of vodka or a snit of whiskey—that will help to make you an expert. And you'll capture the fun and romance of mixology in everything from the French aperitif to the American chaser.

Alcohol: An intoxicating liquid produced by distilling the fermented essence of grains (such as rye or barley), fruits, or even vegetables (such as potatoes for vodka or artichokes for the Italian aperitif Cynar).

Aperitif: A light alcoholic drink, such as dry sherry, served before a meal to stimulate the appetite.

Bar: A counter where alcoholic beverages are made and served. This can be as simple or as elaborate as desired.

Blend: An alcoholic beverage made from two or more of the same or different distilled spirits. For example, blended whiskey may contain two or more straight whiskeys or whiskey combined with neutral spirits.

Branch water: The term refers to water taken from a creek, which was presumed to be clean and pure. Branch water is usually topped with bourbon.

Brut: Champagne with the least amount of sweetness. It's the best choice for drinking before dinner and during meals or for mixing with liquors.

Chaser: An alcoholic drink that follows another, such as a shot of whiskey *chased* with a beer.

Cobbler: A tall, refreshing light drink. A cobbler is usually composed of crushed ice, wine or sherry, fruit, and mint.

Cocktail: A combination of a base spirit—such as vodka, gin, whiskey, tequila, or rum—and a flavoring such as fruit juice and/or another spirit. Cocktails are usually adorned with some edible fruit or vegetable. It's impossible to credit one person or experience for creating this marvelous sensation of relaxation, satisfaction, and stimulation. Some historians claim that the cocktail is an ingenious invention of Prohibition, when poor-quality liquor was commonly sold. However, Americans were sipping Mint Juleps well before the twentieth century. No doubt Prohibition did whet Americans' appetites for cocktails. People drank behind closed doors and popular hosts tested the legal system by serving guests elaborate liquor concoctions. Oftentimes the spirits were poorly made, and a dash of bitters, citrus juice, or other mixers disguised the taste.

Cooler: A tall drink that combines club soda or ginger ale, wine or a spirit, and a lime or orange peel garnish.

Cordial: A beverage made from spirits mixed with fruits or herbs, originally designed for medicinal purposes. Cordials are sweet and a bit on the heavy side. Liqueurs and cordials are synonymous.

Decant: To pour a liquid, usually a wine, from a bottle into an attractive vessel to get rid of the sediment and/or to get some oxygen into the wine to develop its bouquet. Before you decant a liquid, let the bottle stand upright for several hours so the sediment settles at the bottom.

Slowly pour from the bottle into your container. Stop pouring when you see the debris moving toward the mouth of the bottle.

Digestif: An alcoholic drink, such as a glass of anisette, served before or after a meal to settle the stomach.

Distillation: (With apologies to anyone who slept through freshman chemistry and never wants to revisit it.) The process of purifying or concentrating a liquid by successively evaporating and condensing it.

Dry: When describing an alcoholic beverage, the opposite of sweet. A dry champagne, for example, isn't sweet and a dry Martini has a low proportion of (dry) vermouth.

Fermentation: A natural, chemical process in which yeast converts fruit, vegetable, and grain sugars into alcohol. Wines are the best-known fermented beverage. But since all plant foods contain some sugars, you could, theoretically, produce a fermented beverage from, let's say, rutabagas.

Finger: A drink unit of measure equal to the width of your finger, slightly less than an inch. If you ask for four fingers of whiskey, you'll get three inches' worth.

Fizz: A drink that usually contains gin, fruit juice, sugar, and a squirt of club soda or "fizzy water."

Floating: Layering a drink with more than one spirit. Pousse-Café, a multilayered liqueur concoction, is the classic example. The trick is to use spirits with different weights. The heaviest is poured into a glass first, followed by a lighter-weight spirit.

Hard liquor: A spirit with a high alcohol content, such as gin, vodka, whiskey, scotch, tequila, or rum.

Highball: A mixture of whiskey and club soda served in a tall glass. Highball also refers to a variety of drinks served in tall glasses. Many cocktails, including Gin and Tonics, Screwdrivers, and the Cuba Libre, are highballs.

Jigger: A glass used to serve a small amount of liquor, usually 1½ ounces; also a measuring cup holding 1½ ounces of liquid, although some jiggers have gradations up to 3 ounces.

Lemon zest: The thin, outer, colored part of lemon skin. It contains the essential oils of the lemon without the bitterness.

Light or lite: A wine, distilled spirit, or malt beverage that contains at least 20 percent fewer calories than the manufacturer's regular product or a standard and similar product. You should be able to check the label for the number of calories in the light product and in the product to which it's being compared.

Liqueur: A distilled, flavored, sweet spirit. A liqueur may have the natural taste of the distilled product, such as the orange in Grand Marnier, or an added flavoring, such as coffee in Kahlùa. See Cordials.

Liquor: A distilled rather than fermented alcoholic beverage. Gin and vodka are both made by distilling grains (or potatoes in the case of some vodka products).

Lowball: A category of drinks served in an old-fashioned glass or a rocks glass {so named because the liquor is poured on the rocks (over ice cubes) in the glass}. Lowballs include Scotch-on-the-rocks and Manhattans.

Mix: Measuring ingredients to create a cocktail. If you're not a pro, you'll want to pour alcohol and flavorings into a shaker or container, then into a glass so you get the best-tasting results.

Muddle: A mashing technique for grinding herbs to a paste or to small pieces in the bottom of a glass. You can muddle with a wooden muddler. Avoid metal spoons, which can scratch glasses.

Mull: A warm drink flavored with spices. It can be alcoholic, such as Mulled Wine, or alcohol-free, such as mulled apple cider.

Neat: Liquor served without ice or any mixer.

On the rocks: Spirits poured over ice in a glass.

Pony: A 1-ounce measure. Also a stemmed glass that holds 1 ounce.

Proof: A measure of the alcoholic content of a spirit, which is usually printed on the bottle label. For example, tequila may be labeled as 80 proof. The strength of an alcoholic product is also given as a percentage of absolute alcohol by volume. For example, a brandy label may say 40 percent alcohol by volume. The higher the proof and the higher the percentage of alcohol, the more potent the liquor is.

Punch: A chilled party beverage made in large quantities and served from a bowl. A punch may be fruit- or cream-based and may be light on spirits or deliver enough alcohol to live up to its name.

Schnapps: Any strong, dry spirit, usually made from a grain base. Scandinavians refer to aquavit as schnapps. Middle Europeans call a shot of whiskey schnapps. Schnapps is usually served with a beer chaser.

Sec: Dry, describing a wine product with little residual sugar. However, sparkling wines that are labeled "sec" will probably be a bit sweet to your taste and demi-sec is even sweeter. Use sec and demi-sec sparkling wines as dessert accompaniments.

Shake: Vigorously churning ingredients to mix together. To shake, add ice first to chill the ingredients that follow. Don't pack a shaker; you want space for the ingredients to move around. When the shaker feels icy to the touch, strain the drink and serve. Shaking makes a drink slightly cloudy and shouldn't be done when you want a clear-looking cocktail, such as a Martini. Use this technique for drinks with sugar, cream, or juice.

Shooter: A one-gulp drink, usually a jigger's worth. A shooter can be as straightforward as a vodka or whiskey, served neat, or as complex as the popular kamikaze, a mixture of vodka, Triple Sec, and lime. Shooters are associated with binge drinking.

Shot: A 1½-ounce measure (same as a jigger) or a small amount of liquor (one to two ounces), often drunk in one gulp, like a shooter. Westerns have scenes in which the cowboy walks into a bar, orders a shot of whiskey, downs it in 10 seconds, and is ready for fun.

Shot glass: A small glass, about the size of a man's thumb, that holds a shot of some spirit.

Shrub: Not a bush, but an old-style summer beverage from England. A shrub is a tall, piquant drink of fruit, vinegar, and sugar often combined with club soda.

Simple syrup: Sugar cooked with water to form a syrup used to sweeten drinks. You can buy simple syrup in gourmet food stores or in some spirits shops, or you can make your own. See the recipe in chapter 4.

Sour: A drink that mixes lemon or lime juice, a sweetener, and a spirit. The most popular example is a Whiskey Sour.

Snit: A 3-ounce measure.

Spirit: A beverage made from the distillation of an alcoholic liquid.

Split: A 6-ounce measure. Most often used for champagne.

Spritzer: A light, refreshing drink of white wine and club soda over ice.

Stir: Mixing ingredients a few times with a spoon or rod, just enough to blend the flavors. Use stirring, not shaking for any cocktail, such as a Gin Gimlet, that should keep its clear color. If you've got a carbonated beverage, such as a Gin and Tonic, stir as briefly as possible to keep the bubbles.

Twist: A thin slice of lemon, lime, or orange rind used to garnish a drink such as an Old-Fashioned.

Resources

 ## RECOMMENDED READING

If you'd like to read more about cocktails or the history of spirits, I recommend the following books. Although some of these books are out of print, you're still likely to find them in libraries, used bookstores, or through the Web site, www.amazon.com.

Alexis Lichine's Encyclopedia of Wine & Spirits by Alexis Lichine (Alfred A. Knopf, 1967).

Eating in America by Waverly Root and Richard De Rochemont. (The Ecco Press, 1994).

Highballs High Heels by Karen Brooks, Gideon Bosker, Reed Darmon, and Mittie Hellmich (Chronicle Books, 2001).

RealAge by Michael F. Roizen, M.D. (Harper Resource, 2001).

¡Tequila! by Lucinda Hutson (Ten Speed Press, 1995).

The Ultimate A-to-Z Bar Guide by Sharon Tyler Herbst and Ron Herbst (Broadway Books, 1998).

Vintage Cocktails by Susan Waggoner and Robert Markel (Smithmark Publishing, 2000).

SURFING

Web sites are a wonderful source of information. I can't guarantee the following sites are still in operation, but they're worth a click.

www.cocktails.about.com
Check the link with recipes for homemade liqueur.

www.hotwired.lycos.com/cocktail
If you're looking for drink history, stop here first.

www.cocktailtimes.com
What does it taste like? Check the tasting notes on this Web site.

www.webtender.com
Thousands of drinks, plenty of message-board debates, and tips for bartending await visitors to this site.

www.bacchuscellars.com
This mail-order site for spirits is a great stop when you want to read more about liqueurs. The brands are grouped by flavor. You'll find photos and descriptions of the products. It also features a bountiful supply of liquor.

 ## SHOPPING

You'll find a wealth of glassware, bar equipment, and accessories both on the Web and in retail stores. Here are some of my favorite haunts.

www.pier1.com (and Pier 1 stores)
This is the place for swizzle sticks, coasters, and glassware.

www.abestkitchen.com
For everything from flag-topped toothpicks to vinyl-covered, swiveling bar stools, this is the site. And if you're really seri-

ous about your bar duties, you may want to investigate the portable bars offered at abestkitchen.com.

www.marvelindustries.com
One of the leading manufacturers of bar caddies. Check the Web site to see more selections and retail outlets.

www.toohome.com
A good source for deluxe bar caddies with such bells and whistles as Corian top, lights, and refrigeration.

Crate & Barrel (www.crateandbarrel.com)
This chain of lifestyle stores has elegant glassware, bar salt, cocktail party CDs, and great drink pitchers.

Bed, Bath & Beyond (www.bedbathandbeyond.com)
This discount chain carries the Ice Shaver from Progressive International (for making adult slushies).

Restoration Hardware (www.restorationhardware.com)
The evocative aroma of leather and the glint of stainless steel cocktail shaker are the allure. Also check out the glassware and drink-time music.

Williams-Sonoma (www.williams-sonoma.com)
Although this is the chain for serious cooks, serious drink masters will appreciate it as well for its sturdy glassware and pitchers. You'll also find plenty of linens for bar duty.

Index

INTERNATIONAL CONVERSION CHART

These are not exact equivalents: they have been slightly rounded to make measuring easier.

Liquid Measurements

American	Imperial	Metric	Australian
2 tablespoons (1 oz.)	1 fl. oz.	30 ml	1 tablespoon
¼ cup (2 oz.)	2 fl. oz.	60 ml	2 tablespoons
⅓ cup (3 oz.)	3 fl. oz.	80 ml	¼ cup
½ cup (4 oz.)	4 fl. oz.	125 ml	⅓ cup
⅔ cup (5 oz.)	5 fl. oz.	165 ml	½ cup
¾ cup (6 oz.)	6 fl. oz.	185 ml	⅔ cup
1 cup (8 oz.)	8 fl. oz.	250 ml	¾ cup

Spoon Measurements

American	Metric
¼ teaspoon	1 ml
½ teaspoon	2 ml
1 teaspoon	5 ml
1 tablespoon	15 ml

Weights

US/UK	Metric
1 oz.	30 grams (g)
2 oz.	60 g
4 oz. (¼ lb)	125 g
5 oz. (⅓ lb)	155 g
6 oz.	185 g
7 oz.	220 g
8 oz. (½ lb)	250 g
10 oz.	315 g
12 oz. (¾ lb)	375 g
14 oz.	440 g
16 oz. (1 lb)	500 g
2 lbs	1 kg

Oven Temperatures

Farenheit	Centigrade	Gas
250	120	¼
300	150	2
325	160	3
350	180	4
375	190	5
400	200	6
450	230	8

Yes, You *Can* Cook!

Do you have difficulty finding your way around the kitchen? Do friends order take-out when you announce you're going to cook? Never fear. This cookbook was created just for you! Designed for the absolute beginner, this fun and friendly tour of the kitchen makes easy cooking even easier. In the beginning, you'll learn to boil an egg, and from there, you'll graduate to making simple but delicious meals, step-by-step—everything from breads, salads, and main dishes to cookies, cakes, and yummy desserts. Tasty recipes include:

- Easy Banana Bread
- Lasagna Soup
- Fettuccine Alfredo
- My First Mousse
- And much more!

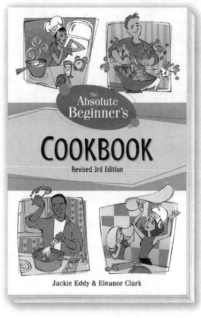

ISBN 0-7615-3546-2
Paperback / 352 pages
U.S. $14.95 / Can. $22.95

Available everywhere books are sold.
Visit us online at www.primapublishing.com.

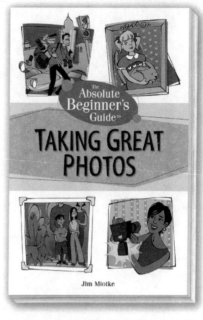